HOW TO RAISE AN ADULT

How to Raise a Boy! Break Free of the Overparenting Trap, Increase your Influence with The Power of Connection to Build Good Men!

Myrtle Hickerson

any fashion for any damages or hardships that may result from any of the information discussed herein.

Additionally, the information in the following pages is intended only for informational purposes and should thus be thought of as universal. As befitting its nature, it is presented without assurance regarding its prolonged validity or interim quality. Trademarks that are mentioned are done without written consent and can in no way be considered an endorsement from the trademark holder.

Introduction

Thank you for purchasing "How to Raise an Adult." You will find a detailed roadmap providing you with the essentials to raise a successful, compassionate, and influential adult within the confines of the pages in this book. Raising an adult starts from the moment the child is born, carving an important pathway of support and acknowledgement paired with expectation and influence. This book will stabilize your ability to provide just that more easily among so much more. I hope you find "How to Raise an Adult" to be inspiring as well as steer you in the direction of raising an incredible adult.

CHAPTER ONE

The Responsibility Of A Child Is Only The Parent's

Parenthood is a magical journey. Whether you are having your own, adopting, fostering, or taking on the responsibility of raising a child that may not have necessarily been yours but was a family member's. Parenthood is also the most important step when it comes to bettering our society as well as raising a successful adult. With parenthood the parent is most specifically responsible for raising that child. The children's wellbeing and proper raising is not a teacher, other family member, or friend's responsibility. When you choose to take on the responsibility of raising your now child it is your responsibility alone.

The first thing you need to realize when you choose to take on the responsibility of being a parent is your child's health, wellness, discipline, and expectations to be met are not determined by anyone else but you the parent. It is also incredibly important to note that how you raise your child can directly impact how they mold into society as well as the decisions that they make you as the parent are responsible for.

Below we will go into detailed descriptions as well as comparisons of different situations to show what responsibility means when it comes to being a parent, as well as how your responsibility can directly impact their probability towards becoming an influential adult.

I have put together four situations to directly implement two scenarios of what can occur when a parent chooses to take responsibility as the parent while also implementing two scenarios where the parent chose not to take responsibility for their child. This is to show and more fully push into effect the important fact that a child's responsibility as well as raising the child flows only to the parent.

- Scenario One:

Jackie is 8 years old. She has been raised from the age of 4 by her stepmother Eleanor due to the fact she had no other family in her life and her father's untimely death in a motor vehicle accident. Eleanor has recently been having issues with Jackie acting out in school. Eleanor immediately schedules a parent teacher conference to find out what exactly is going on with her daughter as well as devise a plan of expectation's for her to do better. In the process of the parent teacher conference, Eleanor discovers that Jackie has been making fun of a few of the other students about their weight, as well as cheating on tests.

Eleanor chooses to look closely at her own life, because she genuinely wants to improve Jackie's life and how the decisions she had recently been making could have directly affected her daughters choices due to her own decisions. She realizes after discussing with Jackie's teacher that she had recently begun dating again as well as fussing over her body shape. Upon further discussion, Eleanor and Jackie's teacher devised a plan because Eleanor chose to take responsibility for Jackie's struggles.

Eleanor also chose to sit down with Jackie to find out her opinion of what had been occurring. Jackie made it clear that she was feeling angry that Eleanor was choosing to date as well as feeling self-conscious of her own boy due to Eleanor showing frustration at her own body shape. Jackie also tells her stepmom that she feels as if Eleanor has not spent very much time with her due to Eleanor's busy schedule.

Eleanor, along with Jackie's teacher, and Jackie put together a plan of action that included being more mindful and kinder to themselves as well as Eleanor and Jackie spending a designated amount of time together.

In this scenario, we see that although Eleanor could have blamed the teacher for her stepdaughter lashing out, she instead chose to devise a plan to work together and how to benefit the child and look at her own actions in the process. Can you look at yourself and honestly see simple things we do as parents on a day to day bases that may be affecting the wellbeing of your child? It is important to note, as a responsible parent you have to have the respect and confidence in yourself to look clearly at

how you are raising your child and come to terms that you are
the only one responsible for that child to mold into aninfluential
adult.

Let's look now at an opposite scenario, where the parent chose
not to take responsibility, instead blaming everyone else around
them for their child's misfortune.

- Scenario Two:

Alisson is 8 years old. Her parentsare divorced, and she is in
Jackie's class. Both her parent's are remarried and are very well
off. When Jackie began acting out, Allison was one of the friends
who instigated her to do so. Alisson's teacher notified both her
parent's Richard and Jane, and both were outraged. They
scheduled a parent teacher as Eleanor did, but continued to not
only barrageeach otherbut also the teacher looking for reasons
as to what the teacher was doing and why she wasn't teaching
their daughter how to act right.

Both parents where also determined that the other individual as
well as their new spouse was the reason for their daughter's
behavior. Neither parent wanted to take responsibility for their
daughter's actions, and instead began pointing the finger in
every direction. When the teacher mentioned sitting down with
Alisson to see what was bothering her, they did not want to
comply instead stating that was the teacher's responsibility.

When the teacher explained her job entails keeping order in the classroom, as well as the education aspect but it is not her responsibility to raise the child nor teach it the morals needed to operate correctly in society, both parents became increasingly irritated and angry requesting to sit down with the principle. They felt their daughter was an upstanding student and that Jackie was the problem in the long run. On all sides, both parties become increasingly irritable and are left with a bigger problem then the start a well as a child who feels unimportant or unheard.

In this scenario we see that although both parent's are equally responsible for raising their child and the actions she chooses to embark on, even if she is influenced by another party they choose to point the finger in all directions but their own. They feel that the responsibility shouldn't be driven back to them, but instead pushed back onto the teacher. In this process their daughter does not go through the necessary support needed for her to feel valued. Whether she was influenced by Jackie or not, if Alisson's parent's had taken on the responsibility and opened the line of communication for their daughter they would have been able to determine the root of the problem and solve it.

In the following two scenario's we will go into detail of two separate situation's of older children. One of which had the support system to cultivate a pathway of acknowledgement and understanding, whereas the other was left feeling as if they do not matter. In both scenarios the children had equal opportunity to have a successful life, but the one was left with a disadvantage do to the lack of responsibility taken by the parent's.

- Scenario Three:

Brandon is 17 years old. His parent's had separated when he turned 13 but had recently rekindled their relationship. Despite the separation both parent's where adamant in their common ground for instilling proper morals and responsibility into Brandon. Brandon is an outstanding classmate as well as head of his high school's performance club.

Despite many situations of peer pressure and opportunities to follow classmates when it comes to doing drugs, Brandon always mentions boldly that he respects himself and his parents. His friends are understanding, but every once in awhile they still ask him.

Brandon feels comfortable enough in his relationship with his parents to talk to them about it without feeling as if he will be judged or chastised. Instead his parents react with support and are avid in Brandon taking on the responsibility to come to them.

When Brandon begins struggling in school, and the teacher comes to them. They handle the situation by taking responsibility for their child and immediately expect an explanation from Brandon. They soon realize that he has been struggling due to them recently dating again after almost 4 years of being separated. They devise a plan together to establish more clear boundaries as well as being more open with each other so that their son can focus more on his schooling instead of being concerned about their relationship.

In this scenario we see again that Brandon's parent's, although they are attempting to rekindle their own relationship, they put their personal issues aside and instead focus on the responsibility of their child. They devise a plan as a family and a working unit to benefit Brandon and his success. Again, they do not blame the teacher but instead look at themselves and what they can do to raise a responsible adult.

Lets look now at our last scenario, which touches bases on a family that depends on the grandparents despite the fact they are the ones who chose to have a child.

- Scenario Four:

Mark is 16 years old. He has struggled with his grades plummeting and barely passing into the tenth grade from the previous year. His parents aregone most of the time and expect his grandmother to deal with him. His dad is often on business trips for a high dollar corporation whereas his mom works for an up and coming digital marketing company.

From the age of 6 Mark has not had much interaction besides his parents coming home and taking him on a shopping spree.

In frustration because of the money driven relationship his parents expect to have Mark continuously puts a strain on his grandmother's health by lashing out and dabbling in drugs along with the inability to hold a successful grade point average.

In every grade level, Mark's parents have repeatedly paid teachers off so that he would move on to the next grade despite his grandmother's frustration. With a lack of support from the parents, Mark is on a downward slope.

Despite his grandmother attempting to take control of the situation, she becomes weary due to Mark's parents blaming her for the way he is acting. The added stress when Mark gets into a fight at school and is expelled because of holding drug paraphernalia leaves his grandmother hospitalized due to a mild stroke.

Mark's parents choose again to blame the grandmother instead of taking responsibility for their child and send Mark to boarding school. This causes Mark to lash out further, immediately landing himself in the wrong crowd and eventually getting caught selling cocaine on school campus where he is taken to juvenile hall. Instead of his parents taking responsibility for these events as well, they blame the school having expected him to be taught how to act due to the high balance they were paying for him to attend.

In the end, Mark struggles with drug addiction and periodically ends up in and out of jail. His parents continue to pay for his bail release and ask themselves what went wrong, searching for who to blame instead of looking at themselves.

In this scenario we see the implications that can arise due to lack of responsibility a parent takes when raising their child. As a successful parent in raising an adult, we have to realize that no one is responsible for your child besides you. As a new parent a lot of raising your child boils down to trial and error, but the best thing you can do when raising an adult is devising a plan that involves taking responsibility.

In all scenarios of raising an adult it boils down to the parents ability to take responsibility for their child's mistakes, misfortunes, success, and implications they go through. You can not under any circumstances raise a successful adult if you choose to focus on an expectation of someone else raising your child. Whether it be a teacher, principle, counselor, family member, or grandparent. The responsibility of raising an adult is determined by the parent alone.

With these simplistic scenarios alone, I have provided clear information of two scenarios that leave us with the reality of what can arise when an adult takes on the necessity of parenthood as a responsible adult, as well as two scenarios where the parents did the opposite, instead expecting others to hold that responsibility. This may seem in some individuals eyes as unimportant, but the responsibility you choose to put forth will determine how important your child feels in your life and what they feel capable of accomplishing.

This goes for all circumstances when it comes to parenthood. Whether you are a grandparent taking on the raising of a child due to unfortunate circumstances, a busy parent trying to make a better life for your child, a parent who has chosen to adopt a child, and so many more circumstances. Parenthood is a blanketed term, but regardless the individual who has chosen to take on parenthood is completely and utterly responsible for raising that child.

A teacher has only the ability to continue building off the foundation that has already been laid by the parents. If you have not instilled discipline into your child's life or a lack of respect, it is not the teacher's responsibility to do so.

Parenthood is one of the hardest jobs we will as adults choose to embark on, and in some circumstances we may be left wanting to hand the reigns to someone else. It is fine to need a break, to take time to yourself, go on a date, take a spa day. But it is never ok to blatantly expect someone else to hold complete responsibility for your child's growth and wellbeing.

In order to raise an influential adult, we need to realize that the way you handle situations and struggles in your life as well as what you are teaching your child is laying a foundation that will directly impact them for the rest of their life. Who you choose to surround your child with, how you choose to raise your child, and the amount of responsibility you choose to take will determine the rate of success your young adult has for the future.

We cannot control every aspect of our child's life or what they end up going through, but we can lay an incredible foundation for them that will provide the skillset for them to impact our society in great ways. In the end, it boils down to the clear fact that in order to raise an adult the first thing you need to realize is you are the one responsible for laying an impactful foundation that will push that child to new levels of positivity they did not even know themselves existed. Take your power back now, by taking responsibility for the raising of an adult that is currently your child.

CHAPTER TWO

The Importance Of Self-Discipline

Discipline is one of the most important tools in your arsenal when it comes to raising an adult, but where discipline is important so is self-discipline. In this chapter we will first go into details of what exactly self-discipline is and determine why it is important as well as how you can show case these abilities in laying a clear foundation for your children's life.

You may have a slight understanding of what self-discipline is, the act of disciplining yourself right? But the term itself goes so much further than that. So, what is self-discipline? This term has a variety of definitions, because it is so vast. Self-discipline is the steppingstone of one taking control of their life. The realization that everyone has the power to control their own urges, wants, and expectations for their life. Self-discipline is the ability to take back the powerthat you originally thought you didn't have and mold your life the way you want it.

For example, an individual who is married and has three children ranging from ages 2-6 chooses to wake up at 3:50 every morning so they can get their blood flowing due to a high intensity workout and finish with a meditation session before anyone in the house wakes up. This would be a prime example and considered self-discipline. They are choosing, despite the want to sleep in because they will be taking care of the family by the time they are done with their workout to instead work on the health and wellbeing of their body.

Self-discipline is the steppingstone for developing influential goal setting techniques as well as an easier way to become successful which we will discuss in a later chapter.

Who can apply self-discipline? Anyone has this capability, we are blessed with incredible minds that are always looking for a challenge to embark on, so in any case any person alive can apply self-discipline to their lives.

Self-discipline is simply put, meant to drive the individual to reach for levels they otherwise would not have known where possible. It is a struggle of the mind and body but meant to reap unfathomable rewards upon accomplishing and taking back control of your mind. Instead of living your life daily without control, self-discipline allows you to take that power back and shape your destiny.

For example, if you are a heavy drinker and it is your automatic habit to come home after a hard days work to sit down and crack open a beer, choosing instead not to purchase beer and have a tall glass of water would be considered self-discipline. You are taking back the power of your inherent habit or urge by doing the opposite and not allowing yourself to succumb to that urge.

I must note, that in order to be successful in teaching your child self-discipline we must first become successful in this venture ourselves. This boils down to the clear idea that for others to follow in our footsteps, we must be willing to accomplish what we are attempting to teach.

How can you become a pro in self-discipline? Everyonecan re-wire and formulate new neuro pathways or habits in their mind. Self-discipline is just that, formulating new neuro pathways that will benefit you further in the long run. In order to find success in this venture, it is important to note our human nature is led by pleasure and pain. I would first start with something simple and apply it daily till it becomes habit while allowing yourself a reward so that your brain associates that situation with pleasure even if it would have originally been something uncomfortable.

For example, if you have been putting off working out but you are struggling to keep up with your children, play games, walk the dog, or anything else of that nature I would apply a daily goal of walking for an hour a day. The important thing to note with this, is not allowing yourself to succumb to the excuses you will inherently hear in your head which could be anything from "I'll do it later" to "I'll start on Monday." Instead choose a time, right now preferably and begin applying yourself with this small goal. As you continue implementing it daily, it will begin to get easier and after roughly 20-30 days it suddenly becomes automatic.

What can you do for a reward of accomplishing something so simple? In order to be successful in applying self-discipline, there must be some form of pleasure in what we are doing. Such as an induvial who has an essay due but has been putting it off due to struggling with procrastination which we will discuss further in a later chapter, suddenly chooses to stop procrastinating and put the time into getting it done. Due to their decision, they can turn the assignment in early. In this case they receive 5 extra credit points they did not know the teacher had mentioned for anyone who turned the assignment in early. They also received a 100% on the assignment, because they were not stressed about the time crunch of getting the work done on time. They allowed themselves an opportunity to absorb the information needed to write a clear and informative essay that efficiently impressed the teacher.

With this example you might ask what their reward was, if you take a close look they not only received a high grade, but an elimination of stress as well as an extra 5 points added due to the self-discipline they provided. This is important because when it comes to your own self-discipline, it is not always something that you hold in your hand that might be your reward. Instead it may be something as simple as the way that it makes you feel accomplishing your goals.

With the example we stated in the previous paragraph of working out, you could implement acknowledging that you took the time to go for a walk, and as a reward you have one cookie. This may seem counterproductive, but you are again applying self-discipline by choosing to only have one cookie. Doing this daily, you begin to feel better, and take control of the situation if you have an issue with working out/eating healthy. Your brain releases dopamine when you receive a reward or do something that makes you feel good which in turn makes you want to do it again. Implementing this into your life daily, you will suddenly begin to see that implementing self-discipline becomes automatic. In fact, eventually it will become something your mind automatically searches for.

The opposite goes for if it's something that inflicts pain. For example, if we take the same situation of working out and implement the fear that your muscles will be in pain or the acknowledgement that you are vastly out of shape. This may be a reason why you don't want to work out, or even something in the office space. Such as writing a report and the fear that you may have not done a good job and will receive a reprimanding from your boss so you instead put it off in that moment out of fear for what your boss will say. Your brain automatically assumes there will be more pain if its completed, whereas if you had applied self-discipline you would have found out and received praise for getting the work done early instead of barely completing it on time.

Self-discipline can be applied to any part of our personal lives, whether that be allowing a certain amount of tv, activity, eating certain foods, completing work, spending time with family, spending time with animals and so much more. Self-discipline is more important then ever in a growing age of technology that we are driven by. With a growing want and need for social media self-discipline is more important than ever to man the most influential part being, once you master self-discipline in your own life you can then tech your children how to apply it in their own day to day life and master raising a happy, healthy, and influential child along the way to adulthood.

How can a child use self-discipline? After all they are only a child, shouldn't they be worrying about playing and hanging out with their friends? Despite this true thought process, most people don't realize that their child is already subconsciously applying self-discipline into their lives. This goes for attending school, eating dinner, completing homework, or getting off from playing video games when their parents tell them to. It is a matter of perspective and looking closely at the decisions your child makes daily. This also goes for constructively guiding them in the direction of turning their subconscious thought process into something to be more mindful of.

Self-discipline most times boils down to doing something we don't necessarily want to do which is something that we inherently do subconsciously daily. Such as brushing your teeth.

You may not necessarily want to, but with self-discipline you do because you don't want your teeth to rot out of your head which is why you also teach that to your children. The reward being you will not loose your teeth. The pain being if you don't brush your teeth you may end up losing them and must get dentures or false teeth.

Applying these techniques to our children's lives as we do our own, gives us the opportunity to take the original subconscious thought process of self-discipline and pull it into the light so that we can directly acknowledge acts of self-discipline. Why does this matter? Because you are then taking back control of your life!

With this in mind, we have the opportunity after taking back our power to teach it to our children. When you bring self-discipline to the light you are laying a foundation for your child to fully apply these techniques to their own life and formulate a pathway towards growing success. Without self-discipline there is no hope of overcoming procrastination or becoming successful, so it is utterly important to begin taking back that power in your life!

How can you apply this to your child's life and raising an influential adult? Just as you began by apply simple tasks such as choosing to clean your house instead of telling yourself you would do it later orhaving the restaurant bag half your dinner so you wouldn't be tempted to eat the entire amount. The same goes for your child. It is ok to expect your child to have responsibilities. This molds them into an influential adult.

After you have taken control and become more mindful of your own self-discipline I would begin by sitting your child down to talk to them about it, depending on their age. If they are younger and it is not really a conversation they will understand, I would instead be more mindful of things there doing such as picking up the toys in their room, eating their vegetables, helping you sort laundry. There are many examples in life that people see as chores or responsibilities that you are giving your child, but instead should be looked at as an opportunity to in stile self-discipline into their lives.

Sitting down with an older child gives you the opportunity to give them constructive criticism as well as inform them of the rewards they can receive from applying self-discipline into their daily activities. Even further to concrete it into your child's brain is the fact if they see you doing it they will follow in your footsteps.

Another incredibly important factor is making sure that you are walking the walk, not just talking the talk. It is your responsibility as the adult and parent to provide a clear understanding of what you not only expect from your child but also expect from yourself. This provides a clear line defined for your child but also holds you accountable as well, which would be another form of self-discipline!

What are some ways a young child performs self-discipline or can perform self-discipline? A child's brain is like a sponge. They react to what they see and hear as well as respond in the same way. They are most importantly molded by what is going on in their life. If they see a parent every single day go for an hour walk at a certain time after turning off the tv, eventually they are going to begin asking questions. This is an opportunity! An opportunity to inform the child why you are doing what your doing, and how it makes your feel to take back that control in your life. It is also important to include examples of how they can apply the same technique. Would they like to go for a walk with you? Did they finish the homework or project that was do? Have they recently cleaned up their room? Did they listen to their friends about ditching school or did they choose to stay in class?

All these examples are life changing depending on what each individuals answers are and will give you more of a first look as to what the percentage of self-discipline they are applying in their own life. It is important to note, although you are responsible for raising a happy, healthy, and successful kid their life is separate from your own. Therefore, their self-discipline and what drives them with certain rewards may be different than your own. In this act, when you choose to apply these techniques you are clearly applying the ability to take accountability for your future as well as your child's and improving your overall capability for developing success.

In all aspects of self-discipline, it boils down to the ability to be diligent in overcoming the short-term reward and instead focus on working towards a long-term reward. Instead of giving in to your urge right in this moment, focus on what you can accomplish as well as the reward you may receive in the long run and apply that technique to your children's life as well. It may be difficult to begin with and seem as if it's child's play, but when it is applied on a daily basis and you become mindful of the actions of self-discipline you take daily in a subconscious manner you will realize just how realistic and rewarding it is.

Self-discipline is one of the most important building blocks in life as raising an adult is concerned. It provides a common ground and stability with a critically laid foundation to support a child's future ventures they will embark upon. With that reality in mind it is important to state how crucial self-discipline is to your own wellbeing as well. Even if you are one who has not mindfully applied this technique into your life or been taught by your own parental figures it is never to late to apply to your own life and benefit from the rewards.

Building Self-Discipline in Teenagers

Now your child has left the 'age of command' and entered the 'age of consent'. Your child now realized that you do not have the absolute power to dictate what he says and does. He also comes to the realization that parents cannot make him do or say anything without his cooperation. It can be an exhilarating feeling to for your teenager to know that freedom of choice lies with him. But it can also be overwhelming at times. The child realizes that he does not have the experience, managerial skills, or self-discipline to handle all of the new found freedom. It can be tough. While he steps out of childhood and transitions into adulthood he will need your support and assistance in learning to become self-disciplined.

The great thing about having a teenager is that their brains have an immense capacity to not just store information, but ponder on it, make reason with it and then turn around and give their opinion or explain the lesson that they have drawn from it. Remember that when speaking with your teen. He is not a child anymore. So try best not to dumb down the conversation. Many teenagers today complain that their parents don't realize they are not children anymore, don't trust them with information, and speak to them as if they are dumb. Of course this is not the parents' true intention. Just as the child is transitioning into a more mature phase of his life, the parent is transitioning as well. The methods they used on their children have to now be tweaked. This phase in the teen's life takes patience from both parties.

Sit your son or daughter down and discuss with them what self-discipline is and what it is not. Most importantly discuss how self-discipline will assist your young person in every aspect of his or her life. After that share the habits of successful people that he or she may look up to in order to encouragement him to develop this vital skill. It may take some research on your part. Take notes and pay attention to the people your child looks up to, whether it is singers, artists, sports figures or actors. Find quotes on self-discipline from these people, share their stories of self-discipline and the outcomes, and share their success.

Below are 5 Habits of Highly-Discipline People:

- Avoid temptation: If your child does not have access to things that would steer him from away from what he has to do, he will find it easier to have self-control. It is much easier to avoid temptation than resist it. Teach them to stay away from the things that tempt them to go off course.

- Change your thinking: Convey to your teen that self-discipline is not self-deprivation. Self-discipline is a means by which your young person can accomplish every goal. It takes focus and hard work.

- Practice self-care: Highly disciplined people take care of themselves. They make healthy life choices to preserve their minds and bodies. You can support your child in these areas by choosing healthy meals for your family, choosing to exercise with your teen as a moment of bonding time, and making sure that he or she is getting the proper sleeping time. Instill in him that it is his responsibility to take care of himself. He only has one body and mind and he must take care of it in order to accomplish any goal he sets out to do.

- Make goals and break them down into smaller chunks:

- Go for it: Whatever your child wants to accomplish, support him, and let him know to just go for it. Some people spend many days, months, and years wanting to accomplish a goal when they are still standing at the starting line. Goals cannot be accomplished if there are no steps taken to reach them.

Always be there to model self-discipline. Give your children some free reign but let them know that you are there to assist and guide. Let them know that you trust them to make good sound decisions. Encouraging comments such as these go a long way.

Building self-discipline in children with learning disabilities

Assisting your child in developing self-discipline skills is a large task. It is even a more difficult task if your child has learning disabilities. You have to take some consideration to your child's abilities, seek guidance from professionals who are experts with your child's disability, and make all caregivers in your child's life aware of the skills you are working on with him so that everyone can be on the same page.

Children with learning disabilities at times have issues with impulse control. This makes it hard to socialize and form friendships. Self-discipline is a skill that keeps our impulses, behaviors and emotions in check.

"Some kids with certain learning and attention issues have a hard time controlling their impulses. They're not being impulsive on purpose." – Lexi Walters Wright

For most people obtaining self-discipline skills begins in early childhood and continues through the twenties. As the child gets older and more mature, his self-discipline increases. But some children with learning and attention issues have a hard time controlling their impulses. They don't do this on purpose. They just have not developed impulse control skills. This is one of the main symptoms of children with ADHD.

If your child has difficulty with self-discipline and it is hard for him to control his impulses, don't think all is lost. There are techniques you can use with your child to assist them with better self-control skills:

- Be clear about expectations: Sometimes a child behaves badly because he is confused about what exactly it is he is supposed to be doing. Let him know clearly what you expect of him. Have him repeat what you have narrated so that you know he has understood. This also gives him the opportunity to ask questions if there is a lack of understanding. It is a good idea to prepare him for any changes ahead of time. For example: "We are having guests over tonight. So there will be extra people at the dinner table. Our friends have children your age, so they may want to talk and play with you." This gives your child ample time to prepare for the change in his usual dinner routine.

- Help Identify Feelings: A child may be able to stop himself from having an outburst if he knows what he is feeling. Teach your child statements of self-control. Here are some examples: "I would like that now, but I will wait until later. I'll wait my turn."

- Play self-control: This is good for younger children. When you are out and about play a game of freeze. While your child is performing some other action, say the word 'potato.' This is the word that lets them know they must immediately stop their action regardless of what it is they are doing. These types of games teach children to stop and think before acting which is paramount in obtaining self-control.

- Take a break: Create a quiet place your child can go to calm down when things get out of hand. Not a place for punishment. Make it a nice, cozy place. This teaches your child that there is another option. He does not have to be explosive and he can regain his composure.

Self-control skills take time to develop and if your child has learning disabilities it may take more time than his other siblings or children of his age. Following some of the tips above can assure that your child does get there. You will see after some time a child with better self-discipline skills.

CHAPTER THREE

What Is Success And How Can It Benefit Your Child?

We have now looked at two of the most important factors to raising an influential adult, and without these two factors there would be no hope for success. If you do not take responsibility as a parent which then trickles to your child taking responsibility as well and apply self-discipline to your life you will fail drastically in finding success. But what is success and why does it matter?

Success is a relative term that can be different for the individual based on that persons goals, hopes, dreams, wants, needs, and experiences. Simply put success is not just about finding financial freedom, becoming a celebrity, or even becoming president! Yes, these may be a possibility of success based on some individuals definition of it, but to find what success is to you personally, you must sit down honestly with yourself and ask a few simple questions.

I would highly suggest sitting down at least two times a year to ask yourself these four questions, as our minds change and formulate new pathways depending on what we have gone through or what interests us.

- What do you want out of life or what is your why and drive/aim that pulls you out of bed in the morning?
- What do you want to do in life or what accomplishments do you want to embark on and concur?
- What do you want to give back in life or what will you contribute to society?
- What goals, financial stability, and expectations will make your success a reality?

With these 4 questions, youcandetermine where your alignment lies with your idea or definitions of success and determine which direction you need to get there. Your definition of success and how you accomplish it will also be a building block to your own child's ability for success. How so? Due to the clear and undeniable fact children lead by example, no matter how old they are. They look to their parental figure for guidance and if you have continued to reach higher for your goals and expectations of yourself they will do the same.

Success is the realization that it is ever changing and evolving like we are. Our interests and expectations change monthly or yearly. Just as every cell in our body replaces itself roughly every seven to ten years so goes for our opinion of success. As we grow and develop both emotionally and physically our expectation of success changes.

For some individuals success deals with things more on the materialistic spectrum. For example, a woman who grew up with two wealthy parents and built her own law firm labeled her success as: "Having an abundant flow of money into my account, an exuberant amount of clientele for my busy law firm, and being able to go on vacation whenever I want while also buying whatever I feel like in that minute."

Whereas in other individuals their rate of success might be more determined by emotions and the ability to spend time with their family. For example: Michael recently had a baby and has started his own business venture, but because his wife is on maternity leave he must focus on working in the construction field to makeup the loss of money. The reason he started his own business venture was because he felt like he was being drug through the mud at his previous place of employment while also being stuck away from his family and two other children.Michael feels like a failure because he must spend time at work and when he is not at work, he is then focussed on building his business. Michael's success is determined by his ability to provide for his family as well as spend time with his family at home. When that is taken away, his vision of success plummets and he feels like a failure.

In another case, an individual may measure their ability to become successful on the amount of extravagant vacations they go on. For example, Jackie is in a committed relationship, and both she and her boyfriend go on monthly vacations to varying places. They recently became engaged and are planning to do a destination wedding so they can add another vacation to their bucket list. When Jackie was asked what her opinion of success was she replied, "I want to be able to have more memories traveling then in my own house."

When it comes to success it is incredibly important to note, whether you are striving for success for yourself or success of raising an influential adult every person is individualized in what encourages them to be successful. This is also meant to say no one thing is right as far as your own personal motivation is concerned. Ask yourself honestly: Are you more driven by financial reward? Seeing a high balance in your bank account? Purchasing materialistic things? Going on vacation? Spending time with family? Having a series of impactful emotions being met?

With each of these it gives you a clearer roadmap of the type of goals you should be setting foryourself to become successful, but how does that tie into raising an adult? As parents, we want our children to have the best opportunity possible to become successful. Realizing what we expect from ourselves and what we deem as success may give a clearer example of what our child may expect from themselves due to the fact they lead by example. Not only that, but if you have answered honestly to yourself you have more clear expectations and a foundation you are working on or are familiar with so that you can then sit down with your child to determine what their definition of success is.

This could be something as simple as sitting down with your eight-year-old to find out what they want to be when they grow up. Or something as important as finding out what their opinion is of success when it comes to doing chores. In a similarity of self-discipline, you can apply success to all aspects of your life and therefore can determine what is going to best work for your child.

In the scenario's listed below, to put it more into perspective I have collaborated three different cases of children and what they deem as their success ranging in ages twelve to seventeen. In these scenarios we can more easily see what motivates our children when it comes to raising a healthy, happy, and successful adult.

- Scenario One:

Alina Morse is fourteen years old. She has always been told by both her parents that she could accomplish anything she set her mind to. When she chose to go to the bank with her father at just seven years old, the teller offered her a lollipop. Alina refused due to the fact her parents had always told her that candy was terrible for a child's teeth. With this realization she asked her father why they couldn't develop a candy or sucker that could prove to be healthy for children's teeth and fight cavities. Due to this analogy, her family developed a healthy version of a sucker that fight's cavities called a "Zollipop." With this idea and goal of success in mind to provide a healthier candy for all children, Alina and her parents where able to build a successful business. The "Zollipop" is now available at most retailersand Alina has a net worth of over 2 million dollars.

Looking closely at this scenario, we can determine that Alina's goal of success was not led by financial gain but to provide the world with a lollipop that wasn't so terrible for children's teeth. She has been raised in a way to chase her dreams, while also not be driven exponentially by money but instead driven to find success in providing something positive for society.

- Scenario two:

Anton Klingspor is eighteen years old. At just six years old, Anton was attending his parents business venture(a manufacturing company) with them choosing to wear a small suit and tie to show his own professionalism. In an interview he mentioned that there is an old picture of himself holding a sippy cup while drinking juice and performing computer coding that his parents had taught him. With this in mind, Anton was obviously destined for his own version of success based on the morals and education instilled by his parents. By the time Anton was the age fourteen he had developed a software that his classmates could purchase so they no longer had to purchase the popular Yeezy shoe through the adidas website.

Anton also developed several programming techniques like this venture but due to several letters sent to himself to remove his programming software from the web he decided to use his programming financial gain to work towards a new level.By 2016 Anton then developed a company called "Indicina Ventures" which focusses on the main goal to bring light to young entrepreneurs if their ideas are not taken seriously by large corporations or companies. Although the company is dedicated solely to small AI companies, it has a net worth of over $53 million. Even with this ace card in his back pocket, at this time Anton is pursuing a new passion which involvesreceiving his bachelor's and master's degrees in a goal set of a simple four years total for both to be completed.

With this scenario, we see an example of a child led by the visual aspect of his parents contributing to his success. Whether that be that at just 6 years old he was already finding dedication in the way he dressed and knew how to code, or by the time he had reached middle school he was focussed on providing an opportunity for his classmates so they would not have to attempt cutting through the red tape to purchase the popular shoes. It is important to note in this aspect as well he was again led to his success by providing a service that would directly impact his classmates in a positive way.

- Scenario Three:

At the young age of fifteen Keiana Cave found a fascination with the oil spill that had occurred back in 2010 and the efforts accomplished to cleaning it up. With this curiosity Keiana was let to asking a professor at a college she was familiar with if she could use a lab they had to do her own research. After they had complied and her curiosity continued to weigh heavily on her shoulders, she decided to conduct research that contributed to newfound knowledge of the amount of cancer-causing chemicals leaking into our oceans. With his discovery by the time she was 20, she focussed her attention on beginning a startup company to focus on cleaning up the ocean from chemicals to benefit not only the sea life but also the individuals in the world that would be directly impacted by the chemicals. With this startup, she attended a competition for an MIT program and received notice from a Chevron Executive. With this incredible opportunity, she then received financial backing to continue her venture in changing the reality of what had arisen due to the oil spill.

Her company was later acquired after great success by an oil and gas corporation at which point in time she began focusing her attention on developing an over the counter and hormone free contraceptive that recently started earlier this year. She hopes to have as much success with this venture as she found with her previous company as well as the dedication provided to it.

With this scenario, we see again at an early age due to the morals and information instilled in Keiana by her parents she chose a new outlook for her own success. Her drive was again not driven by financial gain. I say this because although its not wrong to have materialistic goals when it comes to yours or your children's ability for success, it is important to have a goal of success that directly collaborates with how you can give back to society. Teaching this at a young age gives your child an ability to find success more easily. Why is this? Because, when you choose instead during your quest of success to focus on what you can give back to society instead of your own personal gains, the world around us tends to automatically provide with little effort. This isn't to say all three of these young adults didn't work tremendously hard for their personal success, but if their mindset was more driven for their own selfish gain they would have experienced more trials and tribulations.

Simply stated, have you ever thought about your experiences when it came to enacting something more selfish verses with a heart of gratitude and want to help those around you? If you have, you have probably also come to the conclusion that one of the most important questions you can ask yourself and your child when discussing their expectations for success is how you choose to give back to the world around you? Asking this will get the gears turning in your child's head molding them to be a more compassionate human being.

This will also lay a foundation of support on your end, showing that you care about their future as well as provide a foundation of happiness for your child by opening their heart to what they can contribute and what they have to be thankful for.

Success is a relative term that molds depending on each individuals needs or wants for what they see in the future of their life. What encourages you to move forward? What gets you out of bed? What is your end goal? What will you do once you reach your version of success? These may seem like trivial questions, but they may very well pave the pathway to your success.You may also want to think about the realization that evolving your goals and reaching for higher levels is always a must when it comes to reaching your success. If we are not continuously evolving, whether that be simplistic ventures or vast changes your success will be fleeting.

With success it is also important to note that with the journey of success comes failure, but if you choose to continue to try and try again no matter what your failures are you will eventually find success. There is no physical possibility of reaching success without at first failing multiple times. This is another incredibly important factor to instill in your child's life. It is your responsibility to build your child up to strive towards success with the realization that their ideas may not work the first time around. This isn't meant to be performed in a way that brings dread to your child's life,but instead bringing to light those errors and tribulations they go through will mold them into the incredibly successful individual they are meant to be!

CHAPTER FOUR

Why Teaching Your Child To Focus Can Benefit Them

With parenthood there is a variety of things that makeup the foundation for raising a healthy, happy, and successful child. Among the importance of these techniques would be educating your child on the importance of using their focus to empower themselves and teach them how focus can benefit them. In this chapter we will discuss in further detail why focus is important and how you can teach your child to apply that focus to their own life.

What is focus? Focus is the ability to take ones attention and direct it at a specific goal or task and complete it efficiently with 100% o your effort. With this in mind, how often and easily do we lose focus on a daily basis? Our world is driven by technology and the reward of sitting down to watch TV. So often our children are easily distracted and lacking in focus due to video games, Netflix, TV, and cell phones among many others. Gone are the days of playing outside in most cases unless we apply ourselves diligently and strive to lead by example. Our world has a rampant diagnoses of ADD as well as ADHD due to the amount of screen time we allow our children to have. This causes a harder ability to focus in school, which can lead to failures that don't later lead to success.

It is our task as a responsible parent to educate our child on the importance of focus and how it can benefit our child into becoming successful. We as parents are in complete control of allowing our children to grow in an inspiring way while also molding them by providing adequate information that will set them up for a successful future. If we choose not to pay attention to our child and instead we ourselves are stuck on our phones with a lack of focus on our children, but this leads to a be lead by example situation that leaves our children stuck to there phones or screen time as well. When we take the time to actually sit down with our children and discuss how their focus can benefit them, we are adding to the foundation that we have built towards raising an influential adult.

How can focus benefit your child? Focus is the driving force towards anyone's success, and ass a basis many studies have recently been done to acknowledge that there is no such thing as multi-tasking. Our brains are incredibly fascinating, but there are certain key points which we can focus on at a time. For example, if you are playing instrumental music while driving it will not affect your driving coordination but if you play something with lyrics and you become unfamiliar with your location people will turn down their music so they can pay attention or focus more easily. This is because the language skills associated with driving are used in the same area of the brain as how we listen to music, so turning the volume down quite literally reboots our brain into the ability of focusing on figuring out our location.

Multi-tasking is the ability to do several things at once.Such as typing an essay while watching TV ordoing dishes while talking to your spouse. In these two circumstances you may feel that you are multi-tasking or are a great multi-tasker but in reality your brain is focusing its energy on the one task that it needs to pay attention to the most. Or even worse is the fact it switches back and forth between the different tasks you are doing. This simply means, that if you have several tabs open on your computer (reading an article, Facebook, email, and a browser) and you are flitting back between those four tabs, although it only takes a few milliseconds your brain is refocusing on each induvial one till you switch it again.

Why is this important to know?Because this means your brain is not putting one hundred percent into the tasks you are completing.

This is why texting/phone usage while driving has been outlawed. Simply because you are using the same side of your brain needed to focus on driving. If you are texting you are unable to focus the attention needed to drive safely, instead your brain is picking which one is more important within a few milliseconds. Therefore, if you think back to a time you talked on the phone or more drastically texted while driving you begin to swerve or don't even see what is passing you by which leads to fatal accidents. Multi-tasking for our children can be something as simple as attempting to have aconversation with them while they are playing a video game, making dinner while fiddling with their phone, or washing the car while trying to play with the dog. Our society continues on a day to day basis to try and complete thousands of things simultaneously on a day to day basis with a lacking focus on one individual thing. This leads to a decrease in productivity and an inability to complete tasks with their best foot forward. Instead, we need to strive towards teaching our children the importance of focusing on one task at a time, so our attention is fully committed to what we are trying to complete.

So many people in the world are unfamiliar with this reality, but it is incredibly important to teach our children. When they are not fully focussed on the task at hand, they are not putting forth one hundred percent. If our child does not put one hundred percent into what they are responsible for accomplishing, they are hindering their ability to become successful.

In another spectrum you have a responsibility as the parent to show how focusing on one activity at a time can benefit your child. For example, if your child is bored in a lecture but has a quiz the next day and chooses to play on there phone while neglecting to study for the test the night before the probability of them failing that test is elevated exponentially. Whereas if your teach your child how rewarding it would be to take notes and listen to the teachers lecture regardless of the teachers monotone, they will receive the reward of absorbing the course work more easily while also receiving the reward of a higher probability of passing their test with flying colors.

Having a laser focus towards what your child is doing can benefit them in the factor they are using self-control to take back the power int heir life. Our brains in this manner, are more able to monitor the information coming in and file it away in an efficient manner that leaves us capable of pulling that information back out when needed.

How can you get this point across to your own child? It is important to note that each child is an individual, so what works for one person may not work for another. I am convinced though this can more easily be waded through by determining if your child is more of a statistical or analytical thinker, visual learner, driven by vocal, or driven by touch.

- Analytical/statistical thinker: When you are sitting down to discus focus with an analytical or statistical thinker it is important (depending on the age) to approach with facts and graphs. For example, statistically speaking 1.4 accidents happen yearly due to a lack of focus while driving due to texting and driving or texting while driving has a probability of over six times more likely to cause an accident. Analytical thinkers need the statistical proof or backing when it comes to the realities of focus. If you approach with this information already in hand, your are approaching from their level and showing initiative that your care about the way they think. In another way of providing statistical or analytical backing, you can mention the various studies that have been recently done regarding multi-tasking and Dr David Meyer, a Psychology professor at the university of Michigan among many other circumstances the pin point the importance of focus and attention on one task at a time considering we only have one brain.

- Visual Learner: When you have a visual learner, this means you or your child learns more quickly and absorbs information more easily when something is drawn out or visually shown to you. With this in mind, sitting down with your child to discuss the importance of applying focus to your life when dealing with a visual learner you can easily put together a slide show with the benefits, a quirky video on adobe spark, or even written poster with bright colors to grasp your child's attention. This will pave the way towards a greater success rate of your child absorbing the information you are attempting to tech them when it comes to the importance of how focus can benefit your child.

- Vocal Learner: With a vocal learner it is important to present videos that provide detailed information regarding the benefits of using and applying focus to your and your child's life. These can be videos with fact checked information you design yourself, discussing things clearly with your child, or even looking up videos/listening to podcasts from reliable resources. A vocal learner is influenced by what they hear, therefore you need to be mindful in the way you construct and provide influential information that your child will be inspired by.

- Learner Led by Touch:This is among one of the most fascinating possibilities of the way your child learns and may be one of the most difficult. With touch, your child needs to be able to feel in some way what you are trying to teach them. It is important to discuss, that touch does not necessarily have to be touching. Touch can also be determined by feeling as well. You can, upon sitting down with your child, discus how focus makes them feeland how it inspires them. Youcan also sit down with multiple materials associated with different types of feelings thatfocusyour child while discussing how they feel when they focus on that object. This will push the inner workings of their brain to absorb the information you are choosing to teach them more efficiently.

With these simple techniques added to your arsenal, you have more of a capability tounderstand more fully how you can provide an efficient way of teaching your child. Please remember that each child is an individual and will learn differently, therefore taking the time to acknowledge your child's specific needs is incredibly important. This is also another opportunity to further provide knowledge into the benefit of focus when you ask your child to pay attention to what type of learner they are, after which you can discuss the focus they just applied with their preferred learning technique.

Why does Focus matter? Can it really benefit you?When you choose to dedicate yourself to a specific project and are one hundred percent focussed on that one project, you are setting yourself up for several things to happen. In several studies that have been performed, it has been proven that focus provides:

1. An elevated feeling and understanding of self: This simply put, means that you have a more dedicated understanding of your own wellbeing and accomplishments while also striving to continue towards your growth and progress.

2. The possibility of feeling more in control: Have you ever scrambled around attempting to get several things done before you have to rush out the door and get the kids to schoolin turn feeling as if the thoughts in your head as well as control scatters away like lose marbles? When you apply focus your are taking back that control which can feel incredibly empowering and inspirational to your own personal wellbeing.

3. More positivity: When you are solely focussed on the task at hand, you are applying and dedicating yourself in a way that makes you feel good. Your brain then releases dopamine and searches for more ways to get that same feeling back again. After all, our brains and bodies are driven by reward. If our reward is the way that positivity makes us feel, then our brain is going to search for ways to rekindle that same experience.

4. Focus brings clarity: When you become determined to establish a more consistent focus you also develop more clarity for your life and goals. This means that things suddenly begin to show themselves in an easier way that stimulates you to work harder towards those goals. Clarity paves the way, providing a clear pathway towards the goal of your success.

5. Improved decision making: As you continue you to build yourself up by establishing a greater expectation of focus, you will notice that you will suddenly have an easier time

making decisions. Its no surprise that an individualsIQ drops due to the implication of multi-tasking, but due to the incredible qualities of our brain we have the privilege of bouncing back and gaining momentum with our wellbeing. A lot of the times when you feel incredibly overwhelmed it feels too difficult to decide, but when you allow yourself to focus on one specific thing at a time, your brain has an opportunity to absorb the information it needs more fully. This gives your brain the ability to analyze the information instead of just getting bits and pieces, leaving you with more open space and a clear head to make the decisions needed!

6. Your ability to problem solve will greatly increase: Due to your increased focus and removal of unneeded distractions you are able to pay attention to the problems at hand, discovering new and creative ways to solve them where before you felt stuck and overwhelmed!

These are just six simple rewards we receive when we apply focus to our lives and can easily be formulated to directly promote not only to ourselves, but more importantly to our children. Our children are like a sponge and absorb the information we are giving them willingly if we present it in a way that makes our children feel as if they are important and backs them away from the ledge of feeling overwhelmed. Focus also in conclusion gives the parent as well as the child the opportunity to clear way the fog the may sometimes fill our brains due to the exuberant amount of tasks we face daily leaving us with a paved pathway as to our route for success. Establishing and putting into perspective the importance of focus is a crucial step to becoming successful due to the fact it is physically impossible to become successful when your child feels completely overwhelmed or as if their brain is frazzled due to the amount of information they are trying to analyze on a daily basis.

As a child they are going through many changes in their own life daily and their struggle truly is real. Encouraging them to focus will set them up to grasp hold of the opportunities that may have originally just flitted by right out of their reach.

CHAPTER FIVE

Procrastination And The Forces Of Limitation It Provides

Procrastination, one of the words we may all know very well and attempt to steer clear from. But, so often people confuse procrastination with laziness.It is important to note that there is a clear difference between being lazy and suffering from procrastination!How often do you choose to procrastinate tasks that need to be completed? This is an important factor when raising an adult and in this chapter we will go into details defining what procrastination is as well as the limitations it can cause not only for yourself but your child's growth and wellbeing.

What is procrastination? What is laziness?Procrastination simply put is the act of delaying a task that needs to be completed by choosing to do something else. When you are suffering from procrastination, you are in most cases choosing to do a task that seems to be easier while postponing the task that will take more effort. Laziness on the other hand is an act of not completing anything. (Just as an example)instead telling yourself you will do it later and choosing to eat potato chips while staring aimlessly into space contemplating bad life decisions.

Procrastination has the power to leave even the most determined individual scrambling around to complete a task that could be something miniscule or incredibly difficult. Comparable to depression in the fact that procrastination can debilitate a person from the successful future they are striving for due to their inability to complete an important task at hand. Procrastination also does not discriminate. You can have a task that is incredibly enjoyable to you, but for some reason you are finding yourself incapable of completing it.

For example: Adrien has been working incredibly hard for a promotion at his collections agency and loves his job. But when his boss extends the promotion to him under the exception that he has to complete three senior sales that week, Adrien begins to fall flat. Where he usually completes six to ten senior sales a week, he is barely able to make two due to the fact he begins procrastinating making phone calls. Instead of the needed phone calls he should be making he focusses on organizing his calendar and past payment arrangements till he is left scrambling and feeling overwhelmed and incompetent for the position.

With any form of procrastination, it may lead to a decrease in productivity in the workplace due to the added sense of stress, sense of loss, frustration, and guilt. This causes a possibility of missing out on reaching your goals and accomplishing greater success. When you use procrastination for a long period of time, you are setting yourself up for a future of failure that does not lead to success due to the fact you lower the bar of expectation inyourself which can then in more severe cases lead to job loss!

Procrastination is the ultimate killer for an individual'ssuccess, and it is important to be honest with ourselves how we can combat it. In turn transferring that ability to overcome procrastination to our children is just as important. There is a silver liner though, considering we have ways to combat procrastination and overcome it. Below we will go into details of how you can combat procrastination in your own life as well as apply that to your children's life and how important it is to recognize the difference between procrastination and laziness.

1. How can you recognize procrastination? What are the signs?

It is important to note when recognizing procrastination that if you are re-organizing your workload or assimilating tasks that are more important in your job, this may not be procrastination. Instead, ask yourself if this is a project you are attempting to put off indefinitely or if you are scrambling to move the workload by switching your focus to avoid doing something. If this is the case then you are procrastinating. Other signs of procrastination may include:

- Filling your day with a series of low priority tasks that don't inflict a serious amount of stress. Although lowering our stress or taking it easy periodically is important you must recognize if this is a habit you have become accustomed to using as a crutch.

- Leaving an important task on your to-do-list even if it is something that is high priority. This can be by talking yourself into ding something else leaving this task on your scheduled to-do-list or simply ignoring it completely.

- Taking the time to read your emails several times over but choosing not to do anything with them or choosing not to respond and being incapable of making a clear decision.

- Starting an important or high priority task, but then choosing to "take a break" and clean the house or make coffee.

- Fill your schedule with a series of unimportant tasks that friends, or family members ask you to complete instead of focusing on the series of high priority tasks you had originally put on your to-do-list.

- Continue to wait or tell yourself you will accomplish the task when you are in the right mood or searching for inspiration.

2. How can you identify why you are procrastinating and why is that important?

If you take the time to determine why you are procrastinating, you are equipping yourself and your child with the necessary momentum to alleviate the pressure and overcome it instead of becoming a victim.Therefore,taking the time to understand why you are procrastinating gives you an easier ability to overcome it. What is some of the reasoning behind procrastinating?

- Are you avoiding a task because you find it boring or unpleasant?

- Having poor organizational skills of the tasks you are needing to accomplish can lead to procrastination due to the fact you feel frazzled and spread thin as if you are not sure what tasks are needing to be completed or what tasks are more on your priority list.

- A lack of confidence can also cause procrastination due to feeling as if you are inadequate or doubts about your abilities. This can lead to feeling overwhelmed, and in some cases people have been known to be more afraid of success than failure.

- Fear is another clear cause of procrastination, the fear of becoming successful may sometimes lead to a person feeling their workload and tasks they will have to perform will increase leaving them to instead procrastinate due to their fear.

- The last indicator of why your are procrastinating is a lack of decision-making capabilities or poor decision-making, which is why it is so important to apply self-discipline. A lack of decision-making or poor decision-making skills leads to the individual feeling overwhelmed and frazzledas well as causing them to put off what they are needing to do.

When you are able to sit down honestly with yourself and determine what is causing the procrastination while also determining if it is do to laziness or not, you can then sit down with your child and discuss it with them as well. It is important in all factors of this book in order to see results we must first apply that growth to ourselves before we will see growth in our child. Once you have become efficient in concluding what is causing your procrastination, you can then elaborate by devising strategies to overcome your procrastination.

3. How can you strategize new ways to overcome procrastination?

Procrastination is a habit that has become deeply ingrained;therefore, this is not something in most cases that can be eliminated overnight. It will take self-discipline which is why we discussed it in an earlier chapter. This gives you a foundation to more easily equip yourself with the strategies listed to overcome procrastination and get the success you want out of your life!Below I have formulate a list of techniques you can apply to your life as well as your child can apply to increase the possibility of succeeding.

- Forgive yourself for past mistakes of procrastination. If you continue you barrage yourself, you will lower your confidence further causing more problems of procrastination. If you choose to forgive yourself, you are making a definitive choice to let go of your procrastination from the past and move on.
- Make a definitive choice to commit to your task. This will give you the necessary determination to succeed in the task at hand.
- Establish a reward to yourself for accomplishing the task at hand. This could be as simple as taking a warm relaxing bath or getting a candy bar. The reward should be determined by the greatness of the task. The harder the task is, the greater the reward should be. This is important because as humans we are again led by pleasure and pain. If you have a task that is unpleasant, having a reward that is greater then the task will give you the necessary armor against procrastination. With a reward, also allow yourself to fully process how good it feels to complete a task as well as discuss with your child why it feels good to complete the task.
- In extreme cases, you may need to ask someone who is close to you to hold you accountable. This will give you a

support system to both give you encouragement and help you to strive against disappointing them.

- Give yourself an opportunity to act as you go instead of allowing things to pile up and feeling overwhelmed leading to a feeling of incompatibility of accomplishing your tasks.

- Take time to rephrase your inner voice or dialogue. We all have a voice that is prominent when we are procrastinating, it's the voice that can give us excuses or encourage us to continue working. Be mindful of your inner dialogue and make a clear choice to use that voice to your advantage.So often our inner dialogue includes stating "I need to do this." Or "I have to do this." The problem with this type of dialogue is it implies that you do not have a choice. If you simply flip that to "I choose to do this." You are giving yourself the freedom and the realization that it is your choice to accomplish the task at hand.

- Choose to minimize your distractions. No matter what the task is, if you are struggling to complete it take the necessary steps to illuminate distractions. For example, if your child is writing an essay for a school project but continues to flip back to their email or Facebook, close out all tabs on the computer, shut off the tv, put on a pair of headphones with instrumental music and get to work. Minimizing distractions and focusing attention follows along the lines of the inability to multi-task. If you attempt to multi-task to frequently, your brain becomes overwhelmed and incapable of determining what to focus on which leads to procrastination.If instead, you choose to illuminate these same distractions and focus on one project at a time you are setting yourself up further for a higher success rate.

With procrastination, so many people suffer from it on a day to day basis and the individual might be affected by it differently. This is also important to note considering your child is an individual and may be affected by procrastination differently than you are.

When you take the time to acknowledge that you are procrastinating and follow the steps listed above you have an opportunity to apply the skills to combat your own procrastination. This will then give you another opportunity to teach your child how they can use this skill set as well in their own life. It is important to sit down with our children with an open mind to discuss what might be bothering them or maybe holding them back due to unfounded fears and the importance of limitations procrastination provides.

The act of procrastination limits our capability for success, because we are focusing our energy on refraining from a task that will push us to the next level of our success. If all our energy is expended on not applying our best effort to completing a task, we lose the momentum needed to become success. With this in mind we then get stuck in a treadmill like mentality of continuing to make the same mistakes. It is important to be honest with not only yourself, but your child as well over the implications that procrastination can provide, but how can you do this?

4. How can you devise a plan of fighting procrastination with your child?

We have now discussed the factors that may cause yours or your child's procrastination, as well as some techniques to combat this detrimental error, but how can you apply this to your child's life as well? You may have completely illuminated your own struggle with procrastination, or you might still be in the clutches of overcoming it, but either way there are a few questions you can ask your child when it comes to procrastination and them overcoming it with flying colors.

For example: Amber has been suffering from procrastination at her new job. She is a program specialist and web designer. Amber has recently had an opportunity to show case her tremendous skill set in developing outstanding websites, but she feels as if she is incapable of going further. When her boss gives her a website to design that will quite literally make or break the company, she feels completely overwhelmed and out of her element. She has two weeks to complete the website but chooses for the first entire week to take on every project she can that her coworkers ask for help with.

When her boss asks her that Friday how the website is going, she enthusiastically replies that its going wonderful and she is excited as her stomach fills with dread and confusion of how she can get started. Her confidence is completely lacking, despite her skill set and even though she is overqualified for the task at hand, she isn't sure what to do or if she even wants to complete it. As she clocks out for the day Amber is completely stressed and overwhelmed how she will complete the project by the following Friday.

On that Sunday, Elly (Amber's 10-year-old daughter) exclaims she needs to get a poster board and help completing a science project do that Monday morning. In frustration Amber asks her why she didn't say anything sooner as well as why she was procrastinating something that could be so important and asked when the project was originally given to her daughter. Elly shyly exclaims that she was given it the previous week but didn't want to do it because she hates science and was afraid of failing. When Elly asks what the big deal is because her mom always procrastinates things Amber is blown away. A realization hits her that she needs to do better for herself and her daughter.

With both Elly and Amber sighing heavily, they work till late in the evening developing a water filtration science project that Elly ends up being incredibly proud of. Amber then goes online late into the night despite her early schedule to research ways she can overcome procrastination. She begins applying the techniques listed above to her project throughout that week, and although she struggles tremendously she is able to complete the project flawlessly after enlisting several coworkers to hold her accountable.

That following weekend with a drive to provide more stability with her daughter, Amber sits down with Elly to discuss the science project she had neglected and the importance of not allowing procrastination to dictate her life. At this time, she asked her daughter three questions:

1. What do you feel you are currently procrastinating?
2. Why do you feel the need to procrastinate in this task or multiple tasks?
3. Do you think there is a level of pain you are refraining from experiencing due to this task?

With each question, Amber took time to answer as well as provide the example of the website she had developed that week. Elly looks at her with wide eyes and nods excitedly as they devise a plan together to work on their procrastination and become more mindful with holding each other accountable.

It is important to note, although your child is not responsible for struggles that we as the parent goes through on a daily bases, when it comes to explaining something like this sometimes providing examples and an open doorway this allows your child to realize you're also human and they can resonate with you. Why is that important? Because a child is going to be more willing and feel more heard if they can relate to what you are saying. This will give both you and your child more of an opportunity to overcome the tribulation of procrastination.

CHAPTER SIX

Your Fears Become Reality And Spread To Your Children

Fear is an undeniable factor in your life and your child's life. It is inevitable to at some point in time feel fear, but what you choose to do with that fear is the most important factor. Fear unfortunately has the ability to spread like a wildfire. Not only that, but your wildest fears and expectations become your reality. What do I mean by that? In our universe, no matter what your beliefs are like attracts like. As in what you choose to think about becomes reality, so if you are an incredibly negative person you will attract negative things whereas if you are a positive person you will attract positive situations.Fear works the same way as like attracting like, which is why your fears become your reality. Not only can your fears become your reality, but those fears spread to your family and children.

For example: If you are terrified of living in poverty and struggle on a day to day bases just to pay your bills and provide for your family, you will inevitably continue to do so. Everyday, you will walk in fear to your mailbox waiting for more bills then you can handle and continue to ask why? Or what can I do? The energy that you are putting out is that of panic, which then spreads to your family members. Whether you are married, dating, or single. Whether you live with your parents, have full custody, joint custody, or have a full home that fear will spread throughout the entire household.

Children are incredibly perceptive and can see when you are struggling. Looking back, can you think of a time growing up when your parent, parents, grandparents, or any other parental figure was struggling? I know I myself can think of several occasions my worry grew and I felt like the fate of my own parents struggle was on my shoulders as a child due not to them informing me of their struggles but instead sensing it. This can prove to be detrimental to your own child's worth and leave them feeling as if they are incapable of becoming successful. Your fears become not only your own reality, but also your child's.

Fear is also like sticky tar. It spreads slowly, infecting those around it and roots itself deep in our soul causing a vast variety of limitations not only to you but your child. In this chapter we will further discuss how to combat fear most importantly for yourself, if you have complete control of your own fears you have the ability to guide your child to overcome their own.

What types of fear are there? Although we go through stages of fear in all bases of our lives, below we will go into details of the common issues when it comes to fear and how you can overcome them!

1. Fear of change: With a fear of change comes 5 different possibilities for what portion of the cycle you are currently in. It is important to note, in all aspects a fear of change will directly wash onto your child and prove to be detrimental to your success as well as a struggle for them to overcome.

- Discontent: You are incredibly unhappy with a portion of what is occurring in your life. You tolerate the misery because it is comfortable and familiar, leaving you to deal with it momentarily because of the fear or lack of control if you were to fight through the circumstance you are currently in.

- Breaking point: When your level of discontent continues to grow, you will reach a point where you feel so overwhelmed from the misery you are forced into the change you fear. This is where the break comes and feeling as if there is nothing left but to make change due to exhaustion of a dramatic event occurring.

- Decision: You make a clear decision you will no longer be governed by your fears and choose to decide to make a change. You feel a sense of empowerment, that may immediately be re accompanied by fear. This leaves your decision and empowerment feeling short-lived.Instead you begin to feel powerless as if the decision you made is wrong due to the fear you are feeling.

- Amnesia: Your body paralyzing fear may become so strong it causes your current situation to seem not so dark despite your misery. You attempt to talk yourself out of the decision you previously made, and if left unchecked you are left with the situation incapable of taking the steps needed to better your life.

2. Fear of loss: The fear of loss can be associated with death, losing a family member due to a fallout, divorce, breakup, kidnapping, or anything associated with losing something or someone you care about. When it comes to the fear of loss it is a difficult fear to overcome but acknowledging that you do not have complete control for what happens in your life is a starting point.

It is also important to realize the more frequently you focus your attention on something as negative as say your child being kidnapped you are inviting that to occur subconsciously. This may seem daunting, but its not! Instead you should feel empowered and versus spending valuable time in fear for your child's safety which then leads to an overbearing parental figure, focus your attention on the incredible opportunity you have to provide an amazing childhood.

We may not be able to control all aspects of what occurs in our lives and loss can be painful, but we can control the way react and the fears we have. Fear is a sticky slope that will leave you panicked in a fight or flight mentality, especially paired with the fear of loss. Instead turn your attention to what you have to be thankful for in this moment with your loved ones or things in your life you seem to have a fear of losing.

3. Fear of financial burdens: This fear is one of the most crippling when it comes to fears. Considering that fears have the capacity to become your reality, it is important to be mindful and diligent of our thoughts. When you are constantly living in fear and stuck on the possibility of living in poverty, you are not only causing that to occur you are also molding that mentality onto your children causing a possibility of generational poverty. When your fears of lacking in money or a fear of being unable to provide for your family comes to the surface despite the fact you may think your hiding it, your child naturally knows by the energy and stress you are putting out.

Children read our tone of voice, facial expressions, and above all the energy we put out subconsciously. In fact, has your child ever asked you what's wrong as your pacing in the house attempting to gain control of your breathing? This can cause unneeded stress for your child and a negative mentality that can eliminate or water down the capability of their success.Due to this is is important to implement techniques regarding the ability to overcome your fears no matter how valid they seem to be.

In order to understand the types of fears that cause undue stress, it is first important to understand a bit more about stress itself.

Oxytocin & stress

Oxytocin has been implicated in anxiety and depressive disorders with the administration of intranasal oxytocin reducing stressor responses which in turn reduces anxiety and is linked with reduced amygdala activation. Depression Is also associated with altered oxytocin levels. An important study showed that single nucleotide polymorphism (SNP) of the oxytocin receptor gene OXTR (rs53576) involves a guanine (G) to adenine (A) substitution which yielded a positive outlook for the individual in understanding human social behavior. Individuals homozygous for the G allele exhibited an increase in prosocial behaviors e.g. trust, optimism, empathy, an increase in maternal sensitivity, a reduction in the experience of negative emotions and an increase in the tendency to seek social support and engage in effective coping processes during distress. An organism strives for serenity which can be defined as a state in which a body is free from the negative effects of stress through cultivating practice like meditation or yoga.

Depressed individuals homozygous for the G allele of rs53576 showed an increase in adult separation anxiety and individuals who experienced severe childhood maltreatment homozygous for the G allele show an increase in disorganized attachments and emotional dysregulation. Having the G allele of OXTR SNP rs53576 might facilitate an individual's sensitivity to both a positive and negative environment. In genetically engineered mice with increased oxytocin receptors in the lateral septum, it has been observed that there is an increase in fear and anxiety to a negative social interaction. Thus, intranasal oxytocin increases the salience of social cue while using off-label oxytocin to treat mild social unease might result in neutral cues taking on a more meaningful and negative connotation. In social ostracism & OXTR studies, individuals with one or two copies of the G allele seemed to be more affected by ostracism displaying lower meaningful existence & self-esteem compared to their included counterparts and this was less apparent among AA carriers. They also displayed a distinct blood pressure and cortisol profile such that while others acclimated to lab situation even following exclusion, individuals with the GG genotype who experienced ostracized did not. Interestingly, individuals with GA genotype, or the heterozygotes displayed similar psychosocial responses to individuals with the GG genotype but their physiological responses were similar to AA carriers. This may not be all that unusual considering that oxytocin interacts with many other hormones and neurotransmitters so different outcomes/or behaviors (like psychosocial responses versus physiological responses) likely involves oxytocin interacting with different underlying systems.

Types of stressors

Stressors can be defined as any type of stimulus who upon activation by a variety of factors cause stress. There are as many unknown pleasures as there are stressors in life and we encounter them everyday from having a flat tire to having the babysitter cancel or better yet experiencing flight delays. Stressors are usually measured as daily hassles versus major life events i.e. daily hassles like having a flat tire or having the babysitter cancel are less stressful than major life events like the death of a family member. The idea is that each type of stressor releases different types and separate amounts of neurochemicals which affect behaviour and are reflected in how the individual reacts to his or her environment following the experience of the stressor. There are three distinct stages that develop with stress according to Hans Selye:

i)   Alarm reaction: in this stage, the stimulus in the external environment is detected and humans react with the fight or flight response which puts them in a highly alert state. In this state, mammals will exhibit increased autonomic and hormonal activities that maximize the use of musculature. On the other hand, when an active coping mechanism is unavailable in dangerous situations, mammals engage in a response that involves the sympathetic nervous system arousal which is followed by an active inhibition of movement and blockage of blood away from the peripheral system. This response is known to reduce the functioning of the immune system.

ii)   Adaptation: in this stage, the body activates defensive
         countermeasures against the stressor i.e. the body tries to
         adapt to the stressor. For example, when a baby is deprived
         of milk, he or she reacts by crying and though it is a
         negative adaption it is one that is relevant to the stressor

iii)   Exhaustion: the body begins to tire and lower defences at
         this stage. Movements linked with some type of pathology
         or combination of pathologies are experienced. The
         observed responses fall in the category of cardiovascular
         e.g. heart attack, musculoskeletal e.g. joint damage,
         neurological e.g. mental disorder or an internal organ
         disease e.g. prostate cancer

There are three types of stressors which are psychogenic stressors, neurogenic stressors and systemic stressors respectively. In addition, there are characteristics of each stressor to be considered like severity, controllability, stressor predictability, uncertainty, ambiguity, chronicity and allostatic overload. Psychogenic stressors are emotional or mental in nature and have no underlying biological cause thus are deemed to have a psychological cause. Neurogenic stressors are stressors that affect the central nervous system. They do not directly cause damage but through the cerebral cortex stimulus perceived as endangering are sent through the limbic system in the hypothalamus where they activate the nerve fibers of the autonomic nervous system where an operation occurs that results in a fight-or-flight response. Systemic stressors are stressors that are harmful to an individual's internal balance. Often times, neurogenic stressors and systemic stressors occur at the same time and are followed by intense emotions and/or pain. The physical functioning of the body and the mental stability of the mind is impacted by stress as it raises both adrenaline and corticosterone levels in the body which intrinsically increases one's heart rate, respiration, and circulatory systems thus leading to a compression of bodily organs. The damage done to the psyche by stress is why employers hire a performance coach for staff in most high earning, high stress functioning workplaces. Short term stressors are dealt with by acute stress responses in young, able-bodied individuals due to a history of foolproof homeostatic mechanisms. If the stressors remain consistent especially in older, unfit individuals there is the risk of damage to their overall health e.g. chronic disease.

The hypothalamic pituitary adrenal axis

The hypothalamic-pituitary-adrenal (HPA) axis consists of anatomical structures found in the central nervous system and peripheral tissues which control the stress response. It is so called because the major players of the mechanism are localized in the paraventricular nucleus (PVN) of the hypothalamus, the anterior lobe of the pituitary gland, and the adrenal gland. Brain stem noradrenergic neurons, sympathetic adrenomedullary circuits and parasympathetic systems also influence the integration of adaptive response to stress. To defend homeostasis, an organism will release glucocorticoids by the adrenal glands as a physiological change prompted by physiological or environmental stress but it's not all that simple due to the fact that improper measurement of the stress response can lead to physical and/or mental disorders. Production of glucocorticoids is regulated by excitatory and inhibitory inputs to the hypothalamic paraventricular nuclei (PVN), which controls the secretion of corticotropin-releasing hormone (CRH) and arginine vasopressin (AVP) into the pituitary complex. What follows is a release by the pituitary gland of adrenocorticotropin (ACTH) and adrenocortical activation.

Limbic-sensitive stressors, such as respiratory, cardiovascular or immune stimuli which are greater in context of survival value when compared to fear or exposure to environmental stimuli represent "systemic" stressors. Limbic-insensitive stressors gain access to the PVN through a substantiative catecholaminergic pathway involving the brain stem locus coeruleus while the limbic-sensitive stressors are conditioned by inhibitory gamma amino-butyric acid (GABA) containing projections to the PVN from the desire central nervous system structures. thus, we have a feedback system where excitatory inputs to the PVN act on the surface or through an inhibition by GABAergic neurons of the amygdala, hence increasing HPA activation. When the body is experiencing stress, corticotropin-releasing factor (CRF) synthesized from the hypothalamus moves towards the anterior pituitary gland where it binds to the CRF type 1 receptor (CRFR!) which then activates the cyclic adenosine monophosphate (cAMP) pathway thus fostering the release of ACTH into the circulatory system. When there is CRF flowing in the blood, AVP enlists synergistic effects on ACTH release i.e. they combine and this reaction is mediated through the vasopressin V_{1b} receptor. Finally, ACTH in the blood binds to the melanocortin type 2 receptor (MC2-R) in the adrenal cortex where it creates glucocorticoid synthesis. Through intracellular receptors distributed all over the brain and peripheral tissues like IP3, inositol triphosphate and DAG, diacylglycerol;

glucocorticoids are able to regulate physiological events and stop further HPA axis activation which enables homeostasis to be achieved.

Biological stress responses

There are two types of biological stress responses that are important and deemed as our bodily reaction to prevent short-term stressors developing into long-term illnesses. They are the acute stress responses and the chronic stress responses.

i)   Acute stress responses:

The immediate reaction to an acute stressful event involves the nervous, cardiovascular, endocrine and immune systems. These stress responses feature the release of stress hormones to manufacture energy stores available for immediate use and the diversion of energy to tissues that work harder during stress like the skeletal muscles and the brain. Less important activities such as digestion and production of growth and gonadal hormones are halted as white blood cells are activated and migrate to what we call "battle stations". These features are adaptive in the short term during a stressful event.

The stress hormones are produced by the sympathetic nervous system and HPA axis through the process we discussed in the earlier paragraph. What I didn't mention is ACTH stimulates the adrenal cortex to secrete cortisol which, together with catecholamines up the available sources of energy through the breakdown of fats into usable sources of energy and the conversion of glycogen into glucose (remember the cAMP pathway). This is followed by a distribution of energy to the organs who need it the most by increasing blood pressure levels by one of two hemodynamic mechanisms, contracting a group of blood vessels while dilating others. Cardiac responses are thought to mediate active coping by diverting blood to the skeletal muscles through either the myocardial mechanism or vascular mechanism. Finally, the immune system is activated with the macrophages and natural killer cells leaving the lymphatic tissue and spleen and entering the bloodstream where the number of immune cells in circulation has now increased. The immune cells then migrate to tissues at risk for damage through physical confrontation. Constant use of the acute stress response can lead to a maladaptivity in the sense that for example, chronic sympathetic nervous system stimulation of the cardiovascular system due to stress causes sustained increases in blood pressure which overtime can lead to damaged arteries and plaque build-up.

ii)   Chronic stress responses:

Stress hormones linked with chronic stress lower immunity by directly influencing cytokine profiles. Acute inflammatory infections are regulated by proinflammatory cytokines, Th1 cytokines control cellular immunity by enforcing natural killer cells and cytotoxic T cells, Th2 cytokines process immunity by stimulating B cells to produce antibody, which identifies extracellular pathogens to be killed. Intermediate stressors have been found to increase Th2 cytokines which lowers cellular immunity. For more long-term stressors, Th2 cytokines become dysfunctional and lead to the suppression of both humoral and cellular immunity. Due to the fact that immunology is not as strong in older people, it is clear to see why chronic stress is much more of a bigger problem for that age group as they unable to produce antibodies to fight off infections.

Three approaches are to be taken to treat or manage stress namely to reduce or better yet eliminate the stressor, react to the stressor in a different way and relieve stress through a variety of wellness techniques. You can eliminate an environmental stressor by simply removing yourself from the environment or limiting contact with things in the environment that are causing the stress. For instance, if your friends are smoking and you're a non-smoker you can exit the room they're smoking in or tell your friends not to smoke as it's affecting your breathing, thus rewarding your happy hormones. Using either "situational sterotypy" or response "sterortypy" one can respond to stressors however which way they can with the ultimate goal being not to feel stressed. The choice not to react or to react by limiting the blowback of chaos in a stressful situation is one that is learned over time and as the human brain stores the experience of that stressor in its memory. Activities like sleep, transcendental meditation and dopamine-enhancing exercise do a good job of entraining the mind and body to relax instead of overbooking the stress response and in turn reduces the possibility of depression. Taking a vacation is another good example that works for individuals in terms of de-stressing and finding that calm and serene mood one needs after months of tirelessly crunching numbers. It is hypothesized that exercise is responsible for autoregulatory stress reduction through limbic and reward pathways. The body uses these positive exercises and positive thoughts to neurobiologically project on the hypothalamus and pituitary gland which induces a stress reduction through the HPA axis that makes it possible to deliberately cause less stress throughout the body as stress hormones reduced while dopamine, opioids and opiates are endogenously increased. the role of nutrition is something that will be discussed hereafter in this book with relation to happiness but it also plays a minor role in reducing stress as people can literally eat their out when they're stress although your doctor may not advise it; this is more a learned hopelessness situation as you're trying to forget the stress exists completely through eating as much as possible.

There are several ways to overcome your fears now that you have taken the time to determine what might be the underlying cause of them. This applies also to the fact you have now come to the realization that our fears directly spread to our children and can affect them in a negative way. Below we will go into details of how you can equip yourself with new ways to combat your fears!

Identifying Triggers: In order to identify what might be triggering these three main fears, you must first ask yourself what might be triggering you emotionally? When you have determined what is triggering you emotionally and this can be one or multiples, sit down with each individual one and determine how you are reacting to each trigger and if that reaction is appropriate or reasonable. As an example of what triggers to look for I have listed a few below.

- Having to make a change.
- Challenging yourself or taking the time to learn something new.
- Being criticized.
- Failing at something.
- When something unexpected goes wrong.
- When you accidently make a mistake or make a mistake in front of others.
- Being put in the limelight or put on the spot.
- When you choose to procrastinate.
- When you have a set deadline, feel pressured, or rushed.
- When your reputation might be at risk.

These are just examples and you may have other triggers in your own life. It is important to be completely honest with ourselves when discovering what might be triggering us emotionally so that we can then make the necessary changes to combat it. When you have discovered what your emotional triggers are, you can then dive even further again looking at yourself honestly to pinpoint how to process and move on from those fears. This will give you the power to take back control of your life while also affecting your children in a positive way.

For each trigger take the time to sit down while again being honest and answering a few questions for each individual trigger. It is important to treat each trigger as an individual and go through this process slowly instead of rushing through or you may end up struggling again with those same triggers that lead to various states of fear again.

How can I react, or could I react differently?

How can I strive to think differently?

How can I feel differently?

What people trigger me and what are they doing or saying that causes that to happen?

What do I do in response to what they are saying or doing?

What topics of conversation cause a trigger in me?

How do I choose to respond and can I react/act differently?

After you have taken the time to alienate each individual trigger, it is time to put those techniques into play so that we can then begin to eliminate fear from your life. In this way you will no longer have to be afraid of fear controlling you or preventing you from providing a successful future for your child. You will again need to sit down honestly with yourself to discover how to properly remove fear from your life and I have developed a series of questions listed below to help with this.

Can you see how these fears have negatively impacted your life and relationships?

What will happen if you continue to live in fear?

Are you ready to break the cycle and eliminate fear from your life?

Once you have answered these questions, you must then decide which technique to help break the cycle of fear is going to fit best for you and your scenario. Why is this important? Because when you continue to suffer from fear you may act or assume incorrectly to the events you are currently facing. Taking the time to change your perspective will give you optimum opportunity to combat your fears and become successful in overcoming this sticky slope that can transfer to your children. This boils down too two main techniques you can apply.

1. Extreme Pain: In some cases, it take extreme circumstances or a form of trauma for them to break the cycle of fear. In this case you would have a breaking point that causes you to initially say you have had enough and begin making changes. This could be severe financial loss, a detrimental loss of a family member, your child confronting you, a severe accident, the ending of a

relationship, or even having a nervous breakdown caused by a tremendous amount of fear and pressure.

2. Self-Honesty: With self-honesty, this technique is incredibly empowering. This proves you have taken the time to deeply look at what is rooting your fears and have acknowledged it is time for a change. When you come to a perspective or self-honesty you may have a humbling experience that maybe a part of you doesn't want to change, you have grown accustomed or are comfortable with your habits, you maybe addicted to the current situation, have limiting beliefs, or you may have given yourself the excuse that your pain is a part of who you are. With this in mind taking the time to sit down honestly with yourself is an incredible opportunity to take advantage of overcoming the struggle with fear you may currently be suffering from.

When you come to a conclusion of which technique currently applies to your current circumstance, it is important to note in many cases fear is accompanied by worry. When reversed in almost all scenarios worry will turn into fear, whereas fear is directly associated with fear. How can you overcome the worries you may feel so you can implement a successful life? Below I have listed a series of questions which will encourage you to dis-associate yourself with worry so that you can overcome your underlying fears and move on with your life.

- What is the imagine catastrophe you are worrying about?
- Rate this catastrophe in a percentage of one to one hundred of how bad you feel it will be?
- On a scale of one to ten, how likely do you believe the event will actually occur?
- What is the best thing that could happen instead of your current scenario?
- What is more probable of happening?
- If your worry were to end up happening, would you be able to cope with it?
- How can you flip your mindset with the techniques previously discussed to alter your mindset from your worries?
- What can you say to yourself to reassure the fact that your worry is unfounded, and you will overcome it?
- After looking at your worry from an alternate perspective, how likely do you feel this catastrophe will actually occur on a scale from one to ten?

Fear and worry has the power to alter your mindset from positivity and success to an incapability of performing the tasks needed to succeed. In this fact, those fears due to our mindset can and will become our reality. With this in mind, it is also important to remember that the fears you have will in fact transfer to your children. This can prove to be detrimental to their health, happiness, and over all wellbeing. In conclusion it is our responsibility as healthy parents to work on our own growth so the worries and fears we have can be illuminated so as not to affect the lives we are striving to build for our children.

CHAPTER SEVEN

Pessimism Spreads To Your Children

Parenthood is the ultimate responsibility, and with that responsibility we almost need to become superheroes with our children. With this implication in some situations we are left with the reality of fighting pessimism. In this chapter we will further go into details of what pessimism is and how this negative mentality can spread to our children. We will also go into details of why and how pessimism can effect yours and your child's life negatively and how you can apply techniques to benefit yourself positively to alter your mindset.

What is pessimism? Pessimism is an active mindset that reacts in a negative manner. Pessimism is an individual choosing to have a negative outlook on what goes on around them. Pessimism is going through life seeing the glass half empty instead of choosing actively to see the glass half for or that all you have to do is refill it. Not only is this an issue, but a negative mentality can affect the individuals relationships and ability to attract influential people into their life as well as spill onto their child's life. Pessimism is also the number one killer for an individual's ability to be successful and can prove to be detrimental to a person's health.

What are the symptoms that you might be a pessimist? When it comes to acknowledging that you are a pessimist, you may notice that you have a tendency to expect the worst from people, circumstances and situations. You may also notice that your brain automatically resorts to the bad in any situation. This negative mentality then leaches into the rest of the individuals life and can lead to not only health problems for the pessimist but also for their families members. Led by isolation, a fear of interaction with other people, or having a hard time excepting situations that happen to them and taking the time to move on efficiently.

With pessimism comes negative metaphors that prove to do just as much damage as that negative mentality. What are negative metaphors? A negative metaphor is a common phrase we use as humans to express our feelings comparing something unrealistic to get our point across in a unique way. For example, a pessimist may express that "When it rains it pours" or "There's no light at the end of the tunnel." Using metaphors like this to a pessimist is a go to although subconsciously you may not realize it is actually affecting your life negatively. Using a negative metaphor is implying that there is no hope in the world, and if you continue to do so you are attracting more negativity into your life. With this death circle, a pessimist is able to justify their thought process and use of the metaphor by responding "See? Nothing ever works out for me."

Using metaphors when used efficiently can be the most powerful way of altering your life as well as combatting pessimism. Instead of focusing negatively on what is occurring and wasting valuable energy, instead pay attention to your mindset and altering your metaphors to include something more positive has been proving to increase a persons mood.

For example: If you are used to saying "Nothing ever works out for me" I would advise thinking of three things that have worked out for you, such as do you have food on your table? Do you have clothes on your back? Do you have family or friends that care about you? Among many other examples, this is an easy way to cut and use self-discipline to counteract our negative or pessimistic thoughts. When you have gained control of your negativity by replacing your thoughts with practicing thankfulness, you must then replace the original metaphor with something else such as "Everything is always working out for me" Or "The universe always has great plans for me." This will again concrete the goal to remove pessimism from your life. How do metaphors help with this? Due to the fact we subconsciously use metaphors in our day to day lives, we are constantly cycling through a variety of metaphors daily.

It is important to note that several studies have shown that our brains are incapable of determining what is real and what is just thought. Which means that, if you are constantly thinking negatively your brain associates that with your reality and will more frequentlyacknowledge the negative aspects of your life to justify that thought process. This then leads to a continued occurrence of negative events to spill into all aspects of your life including your children's. To further acknowledge how pessimism can be detrimental to not only your own success, but your child's as well, I have put together threescenarios to demonstrate.

Scenario One: In this scenario we will paint a picture of what becomes of a family with a pessimistic mindset.

Clary is Twelve years old. Her dad has been divorced and remarried for six years now. Clary has no relationship with her mother and neither does her father. Her father Daniel and Clary's stepmom have been continuously fighting the last few weeks. Despite the careful way they try not to argue when Clary is around and their attempt to keep it behind closed doors, Clary is still aware of what's going on. Daniel has continuously showed an outlook on life of complete pessimism and repeatedly uses phrases like "I hate the cards life has dealt me." "Why does everything always go wrong?" or lastly "life just wants me to fail." Daniel and Clary's stepmom are fighting because recently Daniel was laid off from his job, and although Clary's stepmom makes enough money as a teacher to support them, Daniel's usual pessimism has reached new levels. Clary is frustrated and upset because she hears her dad and stepmom arguing every night when they think she's asleep.

Daniel alsowakes Clary up every morning to get ready for school and says the same thing; "Baby girl, time to wake up! Lets see what kind of struggles the worlds going to give us today!"

This may not seem like a big deal but with the continuance of negative energy Clary is seeing in both parents and the constant negative metaphors Daniel is using, that soon begins to seep into Clary's life as well. Her mood is affected, as well as her home attitude, attitude with her friends, and attitude with her teacher's. This causes implications flowing into her friendships, a struggle with her grades, and it also causes Clary to have tremendous lack in confidence.

Instead of Clary being excited to greet the day, go to school, and play with her friends, she begins to adapt the same negative outlook as her father. With this negative personality, her friends no longer want to be around her, and Clary begins to feel isolated while not understanding why.

In this scenario, we can determine just how detrimental having a pessimistic attitude can impact your children. It doesn't just affect your life; it seeps into your children's lives as well as the individuals they interact with on a daily basis. This may seem trivial but having a pessimistic attitude can also lead to severe health issues which we will go into details in with the next scenario.

Scenario Two: Brandon is twenty years old. From the time he was a young child he remembers his parents being incredibly negative in their mentality. When interviewed he said that his mom was more vocal in her pessimism than his father. Brandon also stated that in any circumstance anyone became sick his parents would become increasingly anxious and act as if it was the end of the world. This led to several hospital visits throughout his life that resulted into Brandon suffering from being a hypochondriac.

With any circumstance that Brandon doesn't feel himself he immediately goes to the emergency room out of fear and a negative mentality bestowed on him due to his parents. This has resulted in issues with Brandon being able to hold a steady job as well as his own relationships. What friends Brandon does have, joke and call him Mr. Pessimist due to his overbearing negative attitude. The negative atmosphere Brandon grew up in has also led to severe anxiety and a struggle against self-harm.

Due to Brandon's life growing up in the shadow of his parent's pessimistic attitude, it has affected his entire life. Brandon has had several unsuccessful relationships as well as a waning self-confidence and a continued struggle to keep a job. The negative attitude he grew up with directly spread to his own life, molding him to be identical if not worse than his parents. Do to this fact, Brandon is experiencing more struggles in his life that are affected by the negativity his parents displayed throughout the time of him growing up.

We are truly unaware of how detrimental having a negative mindset or a pessimistic attitude can directly affect our children's lives. The way we talk to our children in a negative way, has the power to set them up for success or the power to break them down. It is our responsibility as loving parents even if we feel stuck in a negative rut to take responsibility for our pessimistic attitude and make the necessary changes so as not to directly affect our children.

What can you do if you're a pessimist? There are several techniques you can apply to your life to improve your positive attitude.

This includes:

- Writing a thankfulness journal. A thankfulness journal is a journal to write down positive affirmations of what you have to be thankful for. Several studies have been done to show that our brains are physically incapable of feeling a negative emotion such as; anger, pain, sadness if we feel thankful. I would suggest choosing ten positive things to be thankful for in the morning, and then repeat the same task in the evening. Things to be thankful for could range from the air you breath, having a cell phone, being able to have children, the sun rising, being alive, and so many more. If this technique is applied thoroughly by truly feeling the emotion of gratitude you will almost immediately see a change.

- Inner mantras of the positivity your are seeking in your life. As parents we want what is best for our children and naturally when we find out that our child might be affected by our pessimistic attitude in a negative way immediately causes concern and an automatic need to change. Another way to combat pessimism is by providing yourself with an important inner mantra such as "I have an incredible purpose" Or "Everything happens for my benefit and for a reason" Or "I am being prepared for what I asked for." The important thing with an inner mantra is to remember to choose something you resonate with. Even if its not necessarily something you believe in at that moment, our brains are physically incapable of determining what is real and what is just a thought. Therefore, repeating a mantra daily will more so establish your want into existence.

- Giving yourself time everyday dedicated to your exercise while doing something you enjoy. As parents we are continuously under stress of providing for our family. It is important to recognize that its ok if you need time to yourself. After all, in the long run, it will directly benefit your child's success. Try to establish something that is at a dedicated time every day. Whether that be going for a walk, the gym, yoga, taking the dog out, or even just exercising and dancing in your own house. Our bodies crave movement, and the release of blood flow will also release serotonin and dopamine which are feel good nutrients we need in our brain.

- Getting plenty of sunlight. If you are a pessimist, it may be something as simple as you have a vitamin D deficiency which leads to depression and high suicide rate. This goes for individuals who live in a climate where it is continuously cloudy or raining.

- Taking time to yourself to enjoy and work on something you love to do or have wanted to learn. In the same way our bodies crave movement, we also crave to learn. Taking time to read and participate in things we love or new things to learn gives our brain a burst of positive energy that can impact our children's and our own lives in astounding ways.

- Being open and honest with yourself and the expectations you have for your own success while also coming to terms with your own failures. Life is not out to get you; in fact, it is rooting for your success. It is important to be mindful and acknowledge what your feeling so that you can move on from it, versus allowing it to stew and blow up.

Pessimism is one of the top implications that have the power to remove our children from a successful future. With these techniques, you are instead taking back the power and acknowledging that having a pessimistic attitude is bringing nothing but pain to your life. Not only does pessimism bring pain to your own life, but it expands further into our children's which affects us further in a negative way because we want nothing but the best for our children.

CHAPTER EIGHT

Teach Your Child to be Mindful

Good parents want to make sure their child is developing the skills they will need to thrive. How to do that is not always easy or obvious. One complication is that the skills valued by one generation are likely to be quite different from the next. So, how do we know what skills are worth valuing? Further, how do we teach them to the next generation? Is it even our responsibility to do so? Shouldn't they learn these things in school?

The answer to the last question is probably yes, but there is no guarantee that they will. Since there is no guarantee, the responsibility often falls to the parents. Teaching these skills does not have to be terribly time consuming. It simply requires patience and a little bit of extra work to involve your child in your daily activities. You know what skills are worth valuing because you apply valuable skills to your own success every day. If you feel you have not honed important skills that you should have, now is the chance to learn them alongside your child. The skills you use and the skills you wish you had are the skills worth teaching your child. Trust yourself on this.

Another question parents have has to do with competing with their child's technologically advanced form of entertainment. Parents often feel their competition for their child's attention is their child's game app. Sure, many parents are filled with gratitude that their child's attention can be occupied by a piece of technology. The backlash, however, is when that child's attention cannot seem to be removed from that piece of technology. The purpose of this book is not to tell you how to manage your child's time spent with technology. It does offer activities away from technology that promote mindfulness. It also offers ideas on how to incorporate technology in activities that promote mindfulness. Some game apps involve the activity of mindfulness, but many are designed to be distractions and offer a sense of mindlessness to decompress. It is important that children do enough mindful activities in their use to be mindful when they are older. We all need mindless activities, but our kids should be using their minds while they are in the peak period of mental development. They should also be sure to interact with the world around them and not just the technological equipment in front of them.

You can show your child how to interact with the world around them by doing it with them. This book gives you some fun ideas that may seem mundane, but are helpful guidelines for teaching your child how to explore their surroundings. The idea is simple. Get outside. Look around you. Feel the leaves. Watch the clouds. We know that we should do these things, but sometimes we need a list to check off. Let watching the clouds be on your to-do list!

Another question you might have is: How can I achieve my own mindful practice while sharing my practice with my children? One answer you may or may not have expected from this book is—Yoga! Yoga is a well-known practice meant to improve mindfulness. This book offers you a flow of poses that you can do with your children.

Take the pressure off of your practice. Laugh with your children as you contort your bodies to look like a cow. See who can hiss the loudest as you reshape your body to look like an angry cat. Play with your practice. Listen to your body. Learn with your children.

It is tricky to say for certain that mindfulness can be taught. What we know for sure is that it can be encouraged and practiced. This book should give you answers as to how both of these things can be done. As you read this, reflect upon what you already do naturally. When you come across an activity that seems banal or obvious, ask yourself why it is so prevalent in your life and applaud yourself for doing the things other parents might not even think of.

From your self-reflection, inspire self-reflection in your children. You probably see your children as a reflection of yourself. Why shouldn't you? They are a reflection of you in so many ways. Reflect upon yourself as you work with your child. Encourage their self-reflection and awareness. Mindfulness means being cognizant of even the simplest things. Be mindful of yourself as you nurture your child's mind. Your child will pick up on your mindfulness because, once again, they reflect and mirror you in so many ways.
There are a multitude of activities you can do with your child to improve upon his/her life skills. The activities in this chapter are divided by theme. You will undoubtedly be able to multiply each activity from every theme tenfold. I encourage you to do so. Use these activities as starter blocks and keep building!

The world is a more stimulating place than an iPad if you approach it as such. Show your child how to approach it as such by doing it with them. We get busy. We always feel as though we need to be doing more. You might feel like you should be enrolling your child in a coding class instead of taking them to the park, but make sure you consider both activities to be important. One of the themes from the next chapter is to go for walks. The point of this activity is to get outside and explore the world around you. The list of activities is meant simply to encourage you to make the most of a walk in order to promote mindfulness.

You have the tools in your home, neighborhood, and backyard to teach your children about being mindful and self-aware. You do not need to go anywhere in particular to do these activities. Once or twice an activity in the next chapter suggests that you should go somewhere you have never been before, but the majority of the activities provided can be done in your home, backyard, or neighborhood. You might have to move a few things around in the living room for your yoga practice, however.

Yoga is a great way to stimulate a fruitful connection between mind, body, and one's surroundings in young children who might not be ready to become active in institutionalized sports and other such strenuous activities. This is the perfect example of a theme you could take so far beyond the ten poses offered in this book. The ten poses offered were selected because they promote mindfulness, have fun names that your child will enjoy, and can be easily accomplished without any prior experience of yoga. They have also been ordered so as to give you and your child and easy flow from one pose to the next.

Like yoga or anything else, mindfulness can be practiced and honed; it just takes a conscious effort. Conscientiousness is mindfulness, after all. Your child will mirror your mindfulness. You simply have to do the work to articulate the experience and provide your child with similar experiences. These activities are meant to give you ideas to instigate theses experience and to inspire mindfulness in yourself and your child. Use them well, but feel free to create your own experiences along the way. The point is simply to get started conscientiously.

You'll find that mindfulness/conscientiousness inspires self-reflection. If you have wondered how anyone can teach self-reflection, you've asked a great question. Some people seem to be turned inward. Others seem to be turned outward. We all seem to have the potential to change our gaze, though. As discussed in the previous chapter, it is likely that your child reflects you in an alarming amount of ways. Reflection mirrors reflection. If you practice self-reflection in front of your children, they will reflect upon themselves. If you ask them to self-reflect frequently enough, they will learn to do so on their own eventually.

Self-awareness is an important part of life. Your children become self-conscious at a scary point in their life. We use the word self-conscious colloquially to mean something like bashful or socially anxious. Its literal meaning is essentially to be self-aware—to be aware of one's self as a self. Your child will become self-aware and self-conscious (both meanings now apply) without much warning. It is important that, when this happens, they now how to self-reflect and then speak to others about their self-reflections. This is how we move between turning inward and turning outward. What you will be teaching your child when you inspire mindfulness and self-awareness is how to turn inward and outward.

Some people get stuck in their inward lives. Struggles that result from this are numerous. This can make relationships challenging. It can make holding a job challenging. It could even cause your child problems at school before the previously mentioned struggles even occur. Children that are more comfortable being turned inward struggle to find their voice. Children that are more comfortable being turned outward struggle to find themselves. It is important to know one's self. It is also important to know others. What you'll be teaching your child with these activities is how to move between looking outward and looking inward.

The walks in nature will pull them outward. Assisting you in daily tasks will make them self-aware and test their ability to apply skills to something in the world. Yoga will make them more aware of their own bodies. The point involved in all 73 of the activities in the next chapter is to work with your child to pay attention to themselves and the world around them at the same time. As useful as technology is, it has a tendency to separate us from the world that is immediately around us.

Technology is precisely mediation, which makes it the opposite of immediacy. Technology is a go-between. Someone creates something for us. We do not have to engage in the world directly. We get to do it directly. We may not be able to speak with someone directly, but with a social media app we can speak with them indirectly. We can even spy on someone, making the experience overtly indirect. They don't have to know we are looking into their lives and interests because we can peek into their lives and interests indirectly.

Overall, this book encourages more direct interaction between your child and your world. One point these activities will continue to stress is that you should do your best to involve your child in the activities you do every day. Even though it might be easier to set the dinner table yourself, consider the importance of letting your child be part of the meal he or she eats. Even if having a pet is difficult, consider the life lessons your child will learn from having one. With that in mind, I hope you will have a look at the activities from the next chapter and then go take a walk.

Interacting with Pets

A beloved professor of mine said it was crucial for parents to make sure their children get the experience of having pets. Pets teach us about nature, life, death, and responsibility. Pets inspire questions. Children will want to understand why a hamster would eat its children, why a snake tortures its food, or why a housecat still hunts even though it isn't hungry. There are lessons in nature. Having pets puts those lessons in the living room, or at least, in the backyard.

One activity is imagining what ones pets are thinking. The neatest thing about this activity is that urges us to think about thinking. From this activity, you and your children could discuss questions as in depth as asking what the nature of thought is and whether or not non-human animals do an activity like the one we call thinking. Or, your discussions can stay as light as considering why one's kitten is looking in a certain direction or what it thinks is beneath the blanket when we put our hand under it.

A second activity is imagining how your pets would speak if they could speak English. This activity follows nicely from the previous one. Now that you and your child have discussed desires and instincts related to the human notion of thinking, you can wonder how your kitten (or any other pet) would express itself if it could speak in English. Would it speak in complete sentences or partial ones? Which thoughts would it choose to convey to its owners?

A third activity is trying to communicate with one's pets. Again, this activity follows well from the previous activities. Once you and your child have considered what a pet might think or feel and how a pet might communicate, you and your child should see how you might communicate with your pet. This will allow you to explore the nature of communication and how much of communication is actually linguistic in nature. Of course, linguistic communication is off the table for the most part. The exception might be verbal commands for one's dog like 'sit' and 'speak'. If you happen to have a parrot, language will have a presence. These exceptions notwithstanding, you and your child can explore the aspects of communication that are not linguistic, such as tones and gestures.

Going on Walks

Parents should go on walks with their children; age does not matter. If a stroller or some other aid is necessary, use one. Parents and children should go on walks to talk about their lives and to observe the seasons together. Just like pets, walks inspire questions about nature. Walks are an opportunity for you to teach your children about nature. If they have questions you do not have the answer to, you now have an activity that allows you and your children to learn something together.

One activity while walking is to discuss the trees. Discussions will vary depending on the seasons. If you walk frequently enough, you will be able to discuss the changes of the seasons. Observe the changes in the leaves, if there are leaves. If it is winter, consider what the absence of leaves means for the animals and insects that spend time in trees.

A second activity is journaling. You and your child could bring along a notepad or journal and write down questions you have about plants, animals and trees you see. The other day my mother and I struggled to recall the name for Spanish Broom. It took up much of the conversation along our walk. We were pleased when she finally recalled the name for the lovely bushes filled with fragrant yellow flowers that appear to have bloomed late this year.

A third activity is stopping to smell the roses. Actually, it is stopping to take a closer look at anything that inspires interest at all. Make the mission of a walk the walk itself, not the conclusion of a walk. Find enjoyment in the journey. Take breaks. Stop and see. Stop and smell. Stop and touch. Stop and talk.

A fourth activity that follows from the previous one is to make note of the stops your child makes on his or her own and ask them why they've stopped. Children will naturally get curious about things and stop to get a closer look. The ultimate goal of the previous activity and this one is to encourage stopping to look. The difference is that this activity also encourages you to ask why your child stopped to investigate a particular thing. This is cause for self-reflection. Why does the Spanish Broom interest your child more than the mailbox next to it?

Gardening

Gardening, like pets and walks, inspires questions about nature. Why do certain plants thrive in certain kinds of soil? What determines the color of a flower? Why aren't our tomatoes as big as the tomatoes at the grocery story? Gardening is a way to learn about nature, be humbled by nature, and interact with nature.

One activity is playing with potting soil. It's important that children dig in the dirt. Experience sand, wood chips, or whatever the playground provides. It is also important that children learn the difference between one type of ground and another. You and your child can discover fascinating things about the difference between types of soil and why certain plants thrive in one type of soil, but not another.

A second activity is to look for seeds together and discuss what kinds of plants grow best in yours and your child's location. Discuss how much sunlight you and your child experience. Discuss how much sunlight certain plants need.

A third activity is, of course, planting. Touch the soil. Teach your children how to plant something. Have them label it. Discuss what it is. Continue the discussion previously mentioned as you watch your plant grow together.

A fourth activity is measuring growth. It is incredible to watch things evolve. You can teach your child about evolution (change over time, not Darwin's theory) by recording the growth of your plant. Observe the difference day-to-day and week-to-week. Measure height. Count leaves. Take notes.

A fifth activity is pulling weeds. Discuss the concept of weeds as a metaphor for consumption. Discuss the activity of taking nutrients from other plants and discuss the notion of sharing necessities with others rather than taking as much as possible for oneself. In other words, tell them what makes a weed a weed. Ask them if they'd rather be like a weed or like a plant.

Interviewing Each Other

Sometimes it is hard to ask the right questions. Sometimes an open-ended question like, "How was your day?" is too quickly answered with a single word like, "Fine." The art of the interview is to ask the kinds of questions that require fleshed out responses that bring about new questions. Interview your children and get them comfortable interviewing you. An interview requires self-reflection and mindfulness.

One activity involved in the interviewing process is coming up with the right questions to ask. Ask your child what kinds of questions they would like to ask you. If they can't come up with any, help them. Think about the kinds of questions they ask naturally and remind them of those questions. Guide them through the process of formulating questions. Discuss the difference between open-ended questions and closed questions. Then, have them make a list (or make it for them if they're too young to write) of questions they'd like to ask you.

A second activity that follows right along from the previous one is coming up with a list of questions to ask them. To make this a team effort, ask them what kinds of questions they would like for you to ask them. Or, ask them what kinds of questions they would like to be asked if they were interviewed on Youtube or Snapchat. This requires self-awareness. It asks them to be mindful of who they are and how they wish to express themselves.

A third activity is having your child guess the answers they expect from you before they ask you the questions they expressed an interest in asking. This activity will give them a sense of how human beings tend to anticipate answers before asking them. Ask your child if they sometimes change their mind about asking a question because they determine that they know the answer after all.

A fourth activity is having your child interview you. Make it fun. Use props in the kitchen or living room for a microphone. Or, go ahead and facetime each other. Again, this book is not meant to condemn technology. In fact, it can be an aid in many of these activities. Make the interview fun, but also challenge your child to ask open-ended questions, follow-up questions, and questions that they really would like an answer to.

Being a Good Assistant

Sometimes it takes a little extra work to allow someone to assist you, especially when your assistant is your young child. It is important work to do, nonetheless. When your children show an interest in assisting you, it is best to let them. Assisting you will teach them mindfulness and self-awareness. Any child can be a good little helper. You just need to teach them how; and give them appropriate tasks.

One activity is cooking. If your child is too young to really help you cook, have them count things. If you're making a walnut salad, let your child play with the walnuts by cracking them with their hands or simply counting them. You can tell them you'd like about twenty walnuts for each bowl. Perhaps it will take up more time to have them assist you in this way, but it is important work for them. They are learning how to follow instructions and how to apply the skills they're learning in school to life-skills.

A second activity is fixing something. Even if your child is not yet able to help you fix something, let them be involved somehow. Show them how to use tools even if they aren't quite ready to use them. Tell them the difference between one tool and another. Show them why the tool they hand you won't work as well as the one you asked for. Make every experience a learning experience for both of you.

A third activity is financial planning. When I was young, I watched my mother balance her checkbook. I remember learning all about checks and checkbooks from her. She would do this activity once a week at least and sometimes daily. I found it fascinating. Today, it is more likely that if your child sees you working with your finances, they cannot tell what you are doing. Managing your bank accounts and credit cars can be done on your laptop, desktop, or even your mobile phone. So, your child might not know the difference between seeing you manage your finances and seeing you peruse images on Instagram. It is important that you include them somehow on what you are up to. Your children will have no idea what financial planning is or how it looks unless you show them. Hand them a calculator and have them help you if they're able. You don't need to share financial anxiety with them, but you can teach them what it means to budget appropriately.

A fourth activity is reading out loud. It is good for us to read out loud no matter what age we are. If you are putting an Ikea coffee table together (or anything else that requires reading instructions) have your child read the instructions to you out loud. Anything that requires assembly is a good opportunity to use your little assistant. If your little assistant is learning to read, a great way for them to assist you is to practice reading instructions out loud. Again, it is good to have your child learn how to apply the skills they are learning in the classroom to life.

CONCLUSION:

You have now read through "How To Raise An Adult" and have been equipped with the tool set needed to raise your child in an influential way. With these hidden keys and an added act of applying what has been read, you will be able to not only see a change in your child no matter the age but also in yourself. It is important to state in all circumstances the importance of our roll as the parent and the tremendous power we have to raise a compassionate, influential, and inspiring adult. Although each child is an individual the hidden keys and information provided in this book will leave you with a new ability to see what your actions are truly capable of when raising an adult. I know the roadmap you have been provided with will give you the optimum ability to accomplish the incredible and rewarding task of raising an adult!